Massacre at Camp Grant

MASSACRE at CAMP GRANT

Forgetting and Remembering Apache History

CHIP COLWELL-CHANTHAPHONH

The University of Arizona Press   Tucson

The University of Arizona Press
© 2007 The Arizona Board of Regents

Library of Congress Cataloging-in-Publication Data

Colwell-Chanthaphonh, Chip (John Stephen), 1975–
    Massacre at Camp Grant : forgetting and remembering Apache
history / Chip Colwell-Chanthaphonh.
        p. cm.
    Includes bibliographical references and index.
    ISBN-13: 978-0-8165-2584-3 (hardcover : alk. paper)
    ISBN-10: 0-8165-2584-6 (hardcover : alk. paper)
    ISBN-13: 978-0-8165-2585-0 (pbk. : alk. paper)
    ISBN-10: 0-8165-2585-4 (pbk. : alk. paper)
        1. Apache Indians—Wars. 2. Apache Indians—History—19th century.
3. Massacres—Arizona—Aravaipa Canyon. 4. Indians of North America—
Crimes against—Arizona—Aravaipa Canyon. 5. Indians, Treatment of—
Arizona—Aravaipa Canyon. 6. Aravaipa Canyon (Ariz.)—History. I. Title.
E99.A6C595 2007
973.8'2–dc22   2006032952

♾ Manufactured in the United States of America on acid-free, archival-
quality paper containing a minimum of 50% post-consumer
waste and processed chlorine free.

12   11   10   09   08   07   6   5   4   3   2   1

An earlier version of chapter 2 was published in the *American
Indian Quarterly*, volume 27, numbers 3 & 4, copyright © 2004
by the University of Nebraska Press; reproduced by permission of the
University of Nebraska Press. Chapter 4 has been adapted from
"The 'Camp Grant Massacre' in the Historical Imagination,"
published in the *Journal of the Southwest* 45, no. 3 (Autumn 2003):
349–369.

Publication of this book is made possible in part by a publication
grant from the Charles Redd Center for Western Studies at Brigham
Young University.

The royalties for this book have been donated to the San Carlos
Apache Elders Cultural Advisory Council.

If I were to remember other things,
I should be someone else.
—N. Scott Momaday, *The Names*

Contents

Figures

Tables

Preface

> I ran on up the side of the mountain, to the top, and stayed there.
> Some others who had gotten away were on top of this mountain
> also. It is called *m-ba-ma-guśl-î-he*. The sun was getting really low
> now. We stayed on top of this mountain all night. The next day one
> man went back to the place where we had been dancing.
> He found lots of dead Apaches there.
> —Sherman Curley, Apache survivor, recounted in 1932

> The attack was so swift and fierce that within a half hour the whole
> work was ended and not an adult Indian left to tell the tale. Some
> 28 or 30 small papooses were spared and brought to Tucson as
> captives. Not a single man of our command was hurt to mar the
> full measure of our triumph and at 8 o'clock on the bright April
> morning of April 30th, 1871 our tired troops were resting on the
> San Pedro a few miles above the post in the full satisfaction
> of a work well done.
> —William S. Oury, Tucson ringleader, written in 1885

On the morning of April 30, 1871, a group of Tucsonans and their Tohono O'odham allies killed upwards of a hundred Apaches and stole some thirty Apache children. The Apaches, predominantly of the Aravaipa and Pinal bands, were living as prisoners of war along Aravaipa Creek five miles east of Camp Grant under the protection of the United States Army.

Few if any have denied this basic sketch. But the rest is, as anthropologists are apt to say these days, contested. As seen in the segments above from Curley and Oury, accounts differ in details, tone, and perspective. They are also distinct in more subtle ways, such as the means of their recording and their selective use (or non-use) by later writers to craft stories of the massacre. But these differences, perhaps innocuous at first glance, provoke a series of unsettling questions: How is it that one event can result in such distinct accounts? What do these different versions say about how the massacre unfolded? Why do writers choose one source but not another? How is the past remembered, individually and collectively? Can we ever know what *really* happened? And why should it matter?

This book is about the Camp Grant Massacre, but it is also about how history is made and what it means, how the past is forgotten and remembered. The differing accounts of a single event, like those related by Curley and Oury, are examined to illustrate that history is not simply the accumulation of names and dates but is rather a strategy people use to make sense of where they have come from, where they are, and where they are headed. The differing fragments of information scholars use to understand the past reflect how every account is culturally, historically, and politically charged. Through an interdisciplinary study, this book examines how history is used as a political tool, engages those perspectives previously silenced, reveals the complexity of the 1871 massacre, and finally contemplates why we must study events we might prefer to forget.

Although the book is geared toward college students and researchers, I do not think that writing for the academic world should mean writing to exclude the interested general public. Thus, while building from a solid scholarly foundation, I have aspired to write a concise book accessible to multiple audiences. This goal is important because I conceive of this project not as the final word on the massacre but as a means of opening a discussion. I hope that this book will foster a constructive dialogue about the past, which is all around us, a part of us, even when it goes unrecognized, unexplained, and untold.

Acknowledgments

I gratefully acknowledge the key assistance of the late Jeanette Cassa and her colleagues on the San Carlos Apache Elders Cultural Advisory Council. I could not have conducted this research, too, without the help of Jeanette's colleagues Vernelda Grant and Seth Pilsk. Several tribal members generously agreed to help the project with interviews: Phoebe Aday, Howard Hooke Sr., Larry Mallow Sr., Beverly Malone, Ramon Riley, Rosalie P. Talgo, Stevenson Talgo, and Eva Watt.

Additional support and assistance were given by T. J. Ferguson, William H. Doelle, John R. Welch, Jeffery J. Clark, Catherine Gilman, Anna Rago, Chelley Kitzmiller, Mary Best, Roger Anyon, Sarah Song, Alan Ferg, Diana Hadley, Karl Jacoby, Ian W. Record, Linda Pierce, Sally Thomas, Dylan Cooper, Birgit Jung-Schmitt, Allyson Carter, Jeff Banister, Geoffrey W. Conrad, Karen D. Vitelli, Paul Machula, Jeanie Marion, Homer Thiel, Michelle Grijalva, Mary Ann McHugh, Alan M. Schroder, Joseph C. Wilder, Devon Mihesuah, and Soumontha Colwell-Chanthaphonh. The insightful comments of two anonymous reviewers of the University of Arizona Press also greatly strengthened this book.

Funding for this project came in part from the Center for Desert Archaeology, the Salus Mundi Foundation, and the National Endowment for the Humanities. I was able to write this book while a Fellow at the Center for Desert Archaeology in Tucson and a Visiting Scholar at the American Academy of Arts & Sciences in Cambridge, Massachusetts.

Massacre at Camp Grant

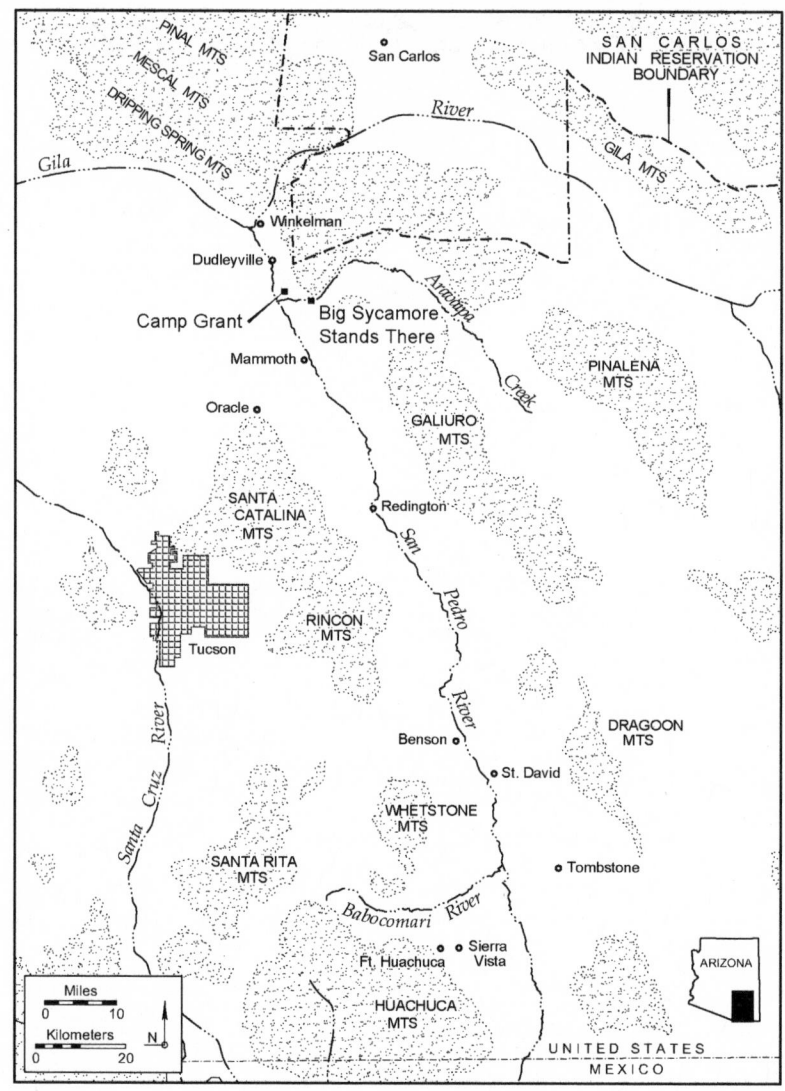

Figure 1. The San Pedro Valley.

PHANTOM HISTORY

The hike up to Wasson Peak begins in an uneven dirt parking lot across from the Arizona-Sonora Desert Museum. A wide trail, an old mining road, starts at the northern edge of the parking lot, then narrows after a mile or so just before crossing a small gully. Below the crossing are dozens of rock art symbols etched into the canyon face by native peoples more than a thousand years ago. In the spring, if the winter rains were heavy, the sides of the trail are blanketed with wildflowers colored in vibrant shades of orange, red, and violet. During the rest of the year, the stands of saguaro and calico-shaded hills are beautiful enough. The trail climbs and then falls, wending to a saddle, a pause before the last mile straight upward. Steep switchbacks pass abandoned mines that are fenced off with barbed wire and have warning signs that dare passersby to enter. Finally, after a long bend is the summit, swept by a constant cool breeze. The view is amazing, unreal, like an image torn from a dream. A perfect panorama sets the scene of desert stretching in every direction. The landscape is not devoid of a human presence, evinced by the creeping sprawl of Tucson, highways, cotton fields, mining pits, and A-10s from the nearby air force base that thunder overhead. Seen from this distance, these marks of modernity seem to blend into the desert, becoming somehow natural, even inevitable. From here, although the traces of history have been left everywhere, it is hard to imagine the world any other way.

Growing up in Tucson, I failed to realize that the history of the Camp Grant Massacre was all around me. I was oblivious to the subtle markers that revealed the origins of my home. As a child

Figure 2. The site of the Camp Grant Massacre.

my school bus drove by Sam Hughes Elementary School, while I attended Carrillo Elementary downtown, just around the corner from Elias Street, Oury Street, and DeLong Street. In the summer, I went to Romero Ruins in Catalina State Park and walked to Romero Pools, where small ponds offered relief from the searing heat. My father and I took an annual pilgrimage to Apache Lake, sometimes taking Highway 77 as it meanders through the San Pedro Valley. Although our car sped by the ruins of Camp Grant, I thought of that drive as passing through just a monotonous, desolate desert. In the quiet afternoons of autumn, I loved to hike Wasson Peak.

These places and place-names were merely the backdrop to my daily experiences. They meant little to me then, but in 2001 I started conducting research on the San Pedro Valley's cultural history and soon learned of the chilling events of the Camp Grant Massacre. My impressions of the familiar names—Carrillo, Hughes, Oury, Wasson, Romero—were transformed as I came to understand the role these men played in the murder and enslavement of scores of Apaches in 1871.

The massacre is not quite what anthropologists call a "public secret" because it is not so much concealed as simply—or not so simply—disregarded. The place-names are, of course, one visible reminder, but scholarly articles, newspaper stories, magazine exposés, and novels about the massacre have also appeared in print over the years. Yet the massacre is not often discussed, debated, or memorialized. Most people I meet in Tucson are like I was: they know little or nothing about the series of events that led to the massacre, its consequences for Apaches, or its role in the foundation of modern Arizona. The massacre is embodied in places like Wasson Peak or the massacre site itself but is also somehow outside them. Even as I have become attuned to this history, it is difficult for me to grasp fully the meaning of these events that occurred so long ago. I have come to see the massacre as a kind of phantom history, a story at once strangely present and absent, palpable yet illusive, haunting places yet never fully inhabiting them, at the periphery of conversations yet just beyond them.

What might be termed the "official" history of the massacre written by scholars, journalists, and novelists over the decades is highly problematic and has in no small measure fostered the massacre's illusiveness.[1] The many essays and books now in print seldom show the complexity of events, often presenting the massacre as an inevitable confrontation between the savagery of Apache lifeways and the heroism of American expansionism. These writings have in effect served to reiterate and reinforce the fictions of Tucson's beginnings, the burdensome duties that paved the way for American civilization. It has been easy for previous writers to present a one-sided view because they have uniformly drawn from material provided by Anglo-Americans deeply invested in the affair, from William S. Oury, who organized the assault, to John Wasson, whose vitriolic journalism validated it, to Lieutenant Royal E. Whitman, who was charged with protecting the Apaches who surrendered. Importantly, the silence of native peoples in these narratives is not due to a paucity of oral histories and traditions. Indigenous accounts survive in archives and in the memories of knowledgeable tribal members. The official history is even more incomplete because it rarely considers the ways in which history itself is a vehicle of power that determines how and why society remembers the past. The resulting limited portrait has consequently rendered the massacre as an event that is *only* past, an isolated happening of little if any relevance to our modern world. In short, then, our current understanding of the Camp Grant Massacre has been clouded by the published literature's reliance on the prejudiced viewpoints of Anglo-Americans, by the degree to which the alternative narratives of native peoples have been overlooked, and by the way the event is habitually seen as disconnected from our present lives.

The Nature of History

That I was raised amid these monuments to the past but knew nothing of the massacre until my late twenties is a salient point of departure for this work. This simple fact inspires fundamental questions about who is empowered to tell history, whose historical voices are heard, and how the past is remembered in the social and political present. Individual and collective memory is an essential part of the human experience, a way for people to shape their sense of self and their perceptions of others.[2] Although remembering and forgetting the past are thus vital to structuring social interactions, these activities are not necessarily harmless. Employed to promote nationalist ferment, justify appropriations of land, and advance agendas of war, history is a form of power.[3]

History is not inherited through the generations but rather is made every day. Although the past is past, how it is recalled or evaded is a strategy played out in the present, a way for people to understand their current condition and explain their vision for the future. The past therefore constitutes a kind of resource used in various social practices. As the anthropologist Marshall Sahlins once wrote, history is not the collection of plain facts but in essence an expression of the present, "value in a temporal mode."[4] The past cannot be recreated any way one chooses, however. Constricted by material realities, cultural logics, and the degree to which interpretations sway others, history is not infinitely malleable.[5] Different communities often seek a kind of negotiated consensus of the past even as historical narratives are perpetually renegotiated, inevitably contested by opposing factions.

Anthropologists have long debated the nature of history in Native

American societies. Late nineteenth-century scholars such as Frank Hamilton Cushing sought to fuse native traditional stories with archaeological fieldwork.[6] By the early 1900s, however, researchers had largely dismissed native narratives as ahistorical, as only fantasy and myth. As Robert H. Lowie famously wrote in 1915, "I cannot attach to oral traditions any historical value whatsoever under any conditions whatsoever."[7] As evidence for his conviction, Lowie pointed to a Nez Perce oral tradition that, he said, grossly misrepresented how the tribe first obtained horses, an event little more than a century old at the time. (The presumption was that since Lewis and Clark wrote down what *really* happened, the contradictory Nez Perce story must necessarily be erroneous.)[8] In the end, Lowie charitably suggested: "The utmost I am able to concede is that a tradition referring to the remote past may furnish a starting-point for linguistic, archaeological, or other investigations; but our knowledge of native *history* will in the end depend wholly on the result of these [latter] inquiries."[9] Thus, in one sweeping statement, Lowie not only discarded native narratives but also elevated Western knowledge, the implied difference being that scholars ground their inquiries on unchangeable texts and objective scientific methods.

Not everyone accepted Lowie's arguments, most notably early American Indian authors who themselves implicitly or explicitly refuted the idea that Indians could only relate myths or legends.[10] The 1960s saw a return to a synthetic approach as researchers demonstrated the historicity, the verifiable historical fact, of oral narratives and also challenged the presumed objectivity of historical texts. Jan Vansina's important ethnohistorical work *Oral Tradition* and his seminal *Oral Tradition as History* presented both the necessary theory and method in order to illustrate that "traditions must always be understood as reflecting both past and present in a single breath."[11] In turn, Hayden White, building on Michel Foucault's theories of discourse, argued that historical texts are inevitably and always partial, an exercise of power because the author is at all times writing from one particular viewpoint.[12] Given these compelling critiques, the most nuanced position today is similar to that of Peter M. Whiteley, who writes that if the concepts of myth and history are to have any merit, they should be "considered *aspects* of how the past is accounted for in *all* societies."[13]

Rethinking the Camp Grant Massacre

In this book I seek to expand the existing literature by coalescing historical documents, Apache narratives, and anthropological texts to provide new insights into the massacre and its causes and consequences. I begin this work with the belief that embedded within every narrative, irrespective of its source, are aspects of the cultural, historical, and political. The methods I use do not require perfectly separating these aspects but rather highlighting them at distinct points in the analysis.

Following this introduction, chapter 2 begins by presenting six unique Apache narratives as a means to counter the official history that has so long silenced native perspectives. This chapter not only illustrates what Apaches experienced before, during, and after the massacre from their own vantage points but also provides an alternative way to contemplate how the past is recalled. Collectively, the Apache narratives establish a markedly different story from the one presented in most articles and books that depend on documents authored by Anglo-Americans. At the very least, they contribute to a more rounded and complete story.

The third chapter builds on the Apache narratives by combining these accounts with ethnographic and archaeological research and an array of documentary sources, including army records, newspaper articles, unpublished manuscripts, and military and civilian maps. This chapter aims to construct a critical multivocality that incorporates multiple viewpoints, not in a celebratory mode but in an analytical reconstruction of past events. "If we are going to tell the whole story of Indian-white relations," Wilbur R. Jacobs wrote some years ago, "we must make an all-out attempt to picture the clash of cultures so that there will be an understanding of both cultures, not just one. . . . What we are seeking, it seems to me, is a wider basis of truth, a better understanding of what has happened in the past."[14] Jacobs's basic argument relates to the work of John Hope Franklin, who once said, "Explaining history from a variety of angles makes it not only more interesting, but also more true."[15]

Chapter 4 acknowledges the way one event can be variously interpreted and broadens the discussion to consider how rhetorical claims about the past are often political. In some regards this chapter concerns what anthropologists call the Rashomon Effect, a phenomenon named after Akira Kurosawa's famous film set in twelfth-century Japan.[16] Few of the basic facts of the story are agreed upon by the film's narrators: after a samurai and his wife encounter a bandit, a sexual act that may be a rape or a tryst occurs, and a death that may be a murder or a suicide. The story is told four times from the perspective of four different characters. Each version purports to be the truth, but clearly each is one-sided and self-serving. Although the term Rashomon Effect was coined to describe the occurrence of variant ethnographic accounts, the movie also emphasizes the problem of the variant narratives offered by participants in any given event.[17] The contested numbers associated with the Camp Grant Massacre illustrate, for example, how the massacre has been recounted in dissimilar ways by participants, their descendants, and later authors. A larger point is not simply that variations exist but that each variation is inseparable from claims of power. "This is the ethical burden of Akira Kurosawa's great film," an anthropologist has recently commented, "not just that the truth of any event is relative to our vantage point and interests, but that the outcome of any event hinges on how successfully we claim final truth for our own view and how we relate our own interests to others."[18]

The last chapter provides a meditation on the meanings of history. This chapter does not focus on *how* the past is remembered so much as *why* it should be remembered. This is an important question because it rouses us to probe our motivations as readers and/or writers of history; it requires us to think about whether the study of such terrible events as massacres is worthwhile or only a kind of metaphorical grave digging, as Apache elder Jeanette Cassa once said to me. I suggest that, in the end, history *is* vitally important because our contemporary identities are inextricably linked to the past. Knowing the past encourages us to resolve inequities that were conceived long ago and that endure today, making the search for the complex truths of past events a search for restorative justice.

Each chapter depends on a variety of evidence and arguments. The overall approach is interdisciplinary, combining anthropology and historiography, and at times archaeology and political philosophy. The documents that support this study are primarily army records and civilian correspondence gathered at archives in Arizona and Washington, D.C. The Grenville Goodwin archives at the Arizona State Museum are a vital source of early Apache narratives. Goodwin was a brilliant ethnographer who conducted research on Apache history and society in the 1920s and 1930s.[19] Sadly, he died at the age of thirty-two, leaving much of his work unpublished. I make use of Goodwin's notebooks, which have not previously been incorporated into any analysis of the massacre. Also important is the current published literature. I pay particular attention to valuable ethnographic investigations few scholars of the massacre cite (for example, a Tohono O'odham version of the massacre Ruth Underhill published in 1938) and little-known writings about the survivors and participants (for example, an Apache account Richard van Valkenburgh published in 1948).

The seeds for this book were planted in 2001 when I began working with four Native American tribes (Hopi, San Carlos Apache, Tohono O'odham, and Zuni) in a three-year collaborative research project on the San Pedro Valley's cultural history.[20] The Camp Grant Massacre developed into a focal point of research for me as it became clear that the topic was in need of novel interdisciplinary research and reinvigorated public discussion. In our ethnohistorical research, my co-director, T. J. Ferguson, and I were able to work with the White Mountain Apache Tribe and the San Carlos Apache Tribe. Research with the San Carlos Apache Tribe predominantly involved the late Jeanette Cassa and her colleagues Vernelda Grant and Seth Pilsk. As I am not myself Apache, the project greatly benefited from Apaches who generously contributed interviews: Phoebe Aday, Howard Hooke Sr., Larry Mallow Sr., Beverly Malone, Ramon Riley, Rosalie P. Talgo, Stevenson Talgo, and Eva Watt. While these interviews are not reported extensively in the chapters that follow, this work provided a crucial means to supplement previously recorded narratives, to get assistance on Apache biographies and place-names, and to receive constructive feedback on the overall project.

These sources of information, which differ in important ways, made this study possible, providing data points for the various perspectives of the groups involved: Apaches, Anglo-Americans, Mexican Americans, and Tohono O'odham.[21] These groups are not only significant for their ethnic associations but also for the degree to which they allow us to comprehend events from the viewpoints of both victims and perpetrators, categories that at times become blurred. The temporal variety of the sources dating from the 1600s to today allows for a diachronic analysis, an understanding of the massacre over a period of time before and after 1871. The sources are also diverse in genre: books, articles, maps, letters, and reports. This textual diversity is beneficial because it illustrates the complexity of how the massacre was constructed and interpreted through time: first by eye-witness accounts, then in contemporary newspaper articles and editorials, then as distant memories, and later as ethnohistorical research, scholarly articles, and novels. The weight researchers and writers have accorded various sources has differed through the years, but Apache narratives have generally been made subordinate to Anglo-American accounts, or more often they have been excluded altogether.

Multivocality and Historicity

A perspective of multivocality, which opens up new possibilities of understanding, also leads in some measure to cacophony instead of harmony—multiple and even conflicting versions of the truth instead of one unified accounting. This is the dynamic that literary theorist Mikhail Bakhtin was trying to capture with the term *multivocality* when he famously used it to describe the novels of Dostoevsky, whose work, he wrote, "is constructed not as the whole of a single consciousness, absorbing other consciousnesses as objects into itself, but as a whole formed by the interaction of several consciousnesses, none of which entirely becomes an object for the other."[22] No simple plurality, multivocality is an *engagement* of different voices arising together to tell a more complete story.

The degree of historicity in any one voice depends on one's frame of reference.[23] As several scholars have noted, Native Americans' stories of days past are often told to community members more to underline moral precepts than to relate historical facts.[24] For when people invoke the past in writing or in oral traditions, they do so to reach different ends that are often more concerned with internal cultural logics than universal claims or undisputed facts. Apache narrators, for example, may be more guided at times by how stories of the past relate to existing understandings of a place or how they can help people live better lives. In the Western scholarly tradition, "history" typically involves the construction of grand chronological and explanatory narratives. Yet, even in the West, history may disregard "the facts." That turkey and cranberries were not served at the first Thanksgiving in 1621 means little to Americans who continue to serve these as essential items of the traditional meal. As we can see, some accounts of the past are commemorative; some are mystical; some mean to describe the past as it truly transpired. Indeed, in this book, rather than constructing a master narrative, definitive and complete, I aim to piece together a mosaic of narratives. By focusing on the collective histories of the massacre, we are able to highlight not just one story but many—not just one voice but a profusion.

And yet such potent issues as land claims, water rights, and the repatriation of sacred objects remind us that there are many times that we need to be deeply concerned about the truth-value of various claims. So the skeptic rightly asks: If all voices must be heard, are not all voices equal? How can we evaluate the truth-value of different perspectives? An appreciation for the varied aims of narratives and a willingness to engage multiplicity does not necessarily lead us down the slippery slope of extreme relativism. Giving *equal consideration* to different voices is not the same as giving them all *equal weight*. As Andrew O. Wiget writes, the problem of locating historicity in oral traditions has long been not the dearth of historical insights in native oral testimony but rather scholars' unrefined analyses that have relied too heavily on the false dichotomy of literalness and myth.[25] Narratives may be tested for their validity, reliability, and consistency.[26] In this approach, validity is the accord between oral accounts and other comparable primary sources; reliability is the uniformity of one person's story over time; and consistency is the agreement among various oral narratives. The concepts of validity, reliability, and consistency provide a sound foundation for an analysis of the historicity of narratives in this book.

Multivocality establishes an advantageous framework for a comparative methodology, one in which multiple fragments of information can be contrasted with many and varied sources. Drawing on Bakhtin, I have tried to focus on the *convergence* and *divergence* of narratives, that is, the degree to which narratives establish similar or dissimilar facts. One example of divergence is conveyed by *bija gush kaiyé*, an Apache elder who survived the massacre. She said in the massacre's aftermath, "They must have killed about one thousand of us, I guess." No other source even comes close to suggesting this high number of victims. *Bija gush kaiyé*'s statement, however, is an *isolated divergence* because the elder's narrative is otherwise consistent with other Apache narratives. In such a case, it would be foolish to dismiss her entire narrative as myth. Instead, we seek reasons for isolated divergence, such as simple error, intentional distortion, misremembering, symbolism, or metaphor. This type of discrepancy contrasts with *structural divergence*, in which one narrative departs fully from another. For example, the story provided by *bija gush kaiyé* in almost no way resembles the narrative of William Oury, who wrote about his experience entirely from the perspective of the attackers. Divergence can notably illustrate how different narratives reveal multiple viewpoints and experiences. Other accounts might verify the historicity in the narratives of *bija gush kaiyé* and Oury, but their stories in juxtaposition reveal very disparate experiences.

Convergence works on the same basic principles. As an example of isolated convergence, consider these two statements that will also be encountered later in the book. They describe the interaction between Apaches and the military in the days leading up to the massacre.

bija gush kaiyé (1932)	Lt. Royal E. Whitman (1872)
The women used to go out and cut hay and sell it to the soldiers for their horses. For this, they would get a red ticket on which they could draw rations or get calico [cloth] and other things.	They were nearly naked, and needed everything in the way of clothing. I stopped the Indians from bringing hay [for free].... I arranged a system of tickets with which to pay them and to encourage them.... the women and children engaged in the work.

These two narratives, when examined in full, are patently different, varying in tone, details, events, characters, and beginning and ending points. But in just this one detail, the two narratives are nearly identical. Since it would be extraordinarily difficult to explain this convergence otherwise, we must reasonably conclude that these narratives articulate (at least) this one historical fact about the system in which Indians gathered hay and traded it for tickets, which they then exchanged for cloth and other items. These disparate narratives, taken together, give us a degree of confidence in this historical fact we might not otherwise have. Finally, structural convergence is exemplified in Oury's two written versions of the event, one in 1879 and one in 1885. These two accounts vary in but a few details; in the overall organization and tone, they converge almost perfectly.

In sum, this book seeks to retrace the Camp Grant Massacre by combining and analyzing an array of new and familiar sources. Through the approach of multivocality, at times I highlight the cultural and political aspects of narratives, while at other times I focus acutely on their historicity. My overarching goals are to study how previously silenced Apache voices portray the massacre, how an array of viewpoints offer novel insights into the massacre and its effects, how the massacre is constructed in the social and political present, and what the massacre means to us today. If I sometimes seem partial toward Apache viewpoints, it is because I hope to redress the 136 years of writings that merely reiterate the partisan language of the very people who committed acts of murder and slavery. Still, I do not advocate re-imaging the massacre exclusively from the stories of American Indians. Rather, I encourage contemplating the event in a broader context that recognizes how multiple interpretations shed light on our shared past. Instead of a single history, the multivocality I propose aspires to engage varying perspectives, to reflect on the past as entangled histories—a mosaic of experiences and remembrances.

They Must Yield or Perish

The attempted extermination of Native Americans in North America can be expressed in terms both broad and specific. In 1491 native peoples, in what is only now the United States, controlled more than 3 million square miles; by 1981 they controlled less than 79,000 square miles.[27] Scholars believe that the population of native peoples in the Americas collapsed by as much as 90 percent between 1492 and 1892; by the end of the nineteenth century, only some 250,000

American Indians survived in the United States.[28] Although a laby-rinthine history is required to explain these dramatic shifts, essentially every colonial power in North America at one time sought outright extermination or the uncompromised assimilation of indigenous peoples enacted through physical violence, disease, dislocation, and social disruption. These goals were achieved through wars, reservations, religious missions, boarding schools, ration programs, and forced relocations.[29] Even in early museums, the compulsion to collect bones and belongings, as seen after the Camp Grant Massacre, reinforced the system that sought to dehumanize and disempower indigenous groups.[30] These programs are not so far in the past: into the late 1800s, sections of the American government and public held that all Indians should simply be killed.[31] The massacres of that era—some 200 dead at Bear River, another 200 dead at Sand Creek, and 150 dead at Wounded Knee—illustrate just how integral brutality was to the mindset of the nineteenth-century American citizenry and its policy makers.[32] By the early 1900s the government had undertaken a more benevolent strategy that called only for the *cultural* extermination of Native Americans. As Commissioner of Indian Affairs Francis Leupp expressed the notion in 1910, "kill the Indian, spare the man."[33]

In recent years controversy has grown as a number of scholars have begun to call the subjugation of indigenous peoples in North America a holocaust and genocide.[34] Critics of these terms typically assert that the government officials, soldiers, and citizens of nineteenth-century America were not trying to decimate American Indians but only doing their best to cultivate peace on a turbulent frontier. Other critics argue that applying genocide and holocaust to Native American history is merely the product of political correctness or excessive sympathies for the plight of native peoples.

However, one day when I was studying the annual reports of the commissioners of Indian affairs from the 1870s, I came to realize that these commissioners would likely be oblivious to all manner of criticism. These men who set the policies and programs of the federal government were shockingly honest and adamant about their intention to wipe out every American Indian group that did not wholly capitulate to the government. They would not, I believe, have recoiled as we do from the concept of genocide. Consider, for example, Commissioner Columbus Delano's words one year after the Camp Grant Massacre:

> No one certainly will rejoice more heartily than the present Commissioner when the Indians of this country cease to be in a position to dictate, in any form or degree, to the Government; when, in fact, the last hostile tribe becomes reduced to the condition of suppliants for charity. This is indeed, the only hope of salvation for the aborigines of the continent. If they stand up against the progress of civilization and industry, they must be relentlessly crushed. The westward course of population is neither to be denied nor delayed for the sake of all the Indians that ever called this country their home. They must yield or perish; and there is something that savors of providential mercy in the rapidity with which their fate advances upon them, leaving them scarcely the chance to resist before they shall be surrounded and disarmed.[35]

This attitude was not momentary, a transitory hatred uttered in war, but part of the broader nineteenth-century American outlook that infused the imperialist zeal for territorial acquisition with the politics of racial determinism. Consider this statement originally published in 1894 in Theodore Roosevelt's best-selling multivolume work *The Winning of the West*:

> The most ultimately righteous of all wars is a war with savages, though it is apt to be also the most terrible and inhuman. The rude, fierce settler who drives the savage from the land lays all civilized mankind under a debt to him. American and Indian, Boer and Zulu, Cossack and Tartar, New Zealander and Maori— in each case the victor, horrible though many of his deeds are, has laid deep the foundations for the future greatness of a mighty people. The consequences of struggles for territory between civilized nations seem small by comparison. Looked at from the standpoint of the ages, it is of little moment whether Lorraine is part of Germany or of France, whether the northern Adriatic cities pay homage to Austrian Kaiser or Italian King; But it is of incalculable importance that America, Australia, and Siberia should pass out of the hands of their red, black, and yellow ab-

original owners, and become the heritage of the dominant world races.[36]

The semantic debate over the language of genocide is at times a red herring that can distract from a consideration of material realities and consequences. Whatever we choose to call it, the extreme social, psychological, and physical violence inflicted upon communities throughout Native America is clear enough. Without diminishing the experiences of other native peoples, it is worth calling attention to the ways that Apaches in particular have endured centuries of misunderstanding and misrepresentation. As discussed in chapter 3, by the 1700s Apache groups were already being portrayed as nomadic raiders, wildly violent, always in pursuit of war. But in well-documented cases in 1793, 1836, and 1866, Aravaipa and Pinal Apache leaders were the ones to sue for peace. No one can deny that Apaches long were involved in raiding and warfare.[37] But they were also the victims of random massacres; we know of at least two before Camp Grant, along Aravaipa Creek in 1793 and 1832. Significantly, Apaches have long been portrayed as *naturally* violent, making it simply good policy for American officials to call for extermination. As John Noble Goodwin, the first Arizona governor, wrote in 1866, the country was demanding a "fair, open and persistent war" until the Apaches "bow their necks in submission" and are placed on reservations "to labor or starve," or until they are simply "exterminated."[38] The Apaches, history books tell us, are the savages.

The Camp Grant Massacre cannot be fully understood as an isolated event, a story that begins and ends in 1871. Although the bridge that spans historical cause and effect is on occasion elusive, the massacre needs to be considered first in the context of colonialism. This introductory discussion need not dominate our view of the massacre, but it does provide a backdrop for understanding the unfinished business of colonialism, the mechanisms of violence that beset the Americas before and since the arrival of Europeans. An extended view of colonialism also helps underscore the idea that violence exists on a continuum: murder and kidnapping are obvious and extreme crimes; less obvious but also injurious are land theft, which undermines a people's autonomy and livelihood, and malicious stereotyping, which ultimately excuses brutality.[39] I am acutely aware that the portrayal of events and peoples has the power to change lives. I therefore present the book with great earnestness, which I invite my reader to share as we explore the making and meaning of Apache history.

The Urge to Forget and to Remember

Memory, its function and expression, is an essential part of what it means to be human. "Our capacity to remember and to share our memories with others is distinctively human," as anthropologist Erika Bourguignon writes, "since it involves the use of language and of other complex representations."[40] Bourguignon notes that it is our ability to discuss the past and share symbols that leads to collective memory, reinforced and sustained by public rituals such as pilgrimages and tangible markers such as monuments. Humans strive to recollect and savor certain events of the past while seeking to suppress and silence others, particularly memories steeped in bitterness. Having lost family in the horrors of World War II, Bourguignon is acutely aware of how "the urge to remember, to fight against oblivion, is in conflict with the urge to forget, to go on living."[41] On subjects like the massacre of Native Americans or the European Holocaust, it is tempting to speak in hushed tones or not at all. As Jadzia Lenartowicz Rylko ended several interviews in which she discussed her surviving the Holocaust, "Let's not talk anymore, because then I don't sleep at night, thinking of all this."[42] Knowledge of such events may lead to restless nights. Leaving the waters of history still and undisturbed is often less difficult than dredging their murky and unfathomed depths. Yet, because individual and collective memories form the basis of our personal identities, everyday lives, and larger communities, we must take up this challenge and confront our often troubling pasts to better understand ourselves.

TRADITIONAL HISTORY

In 1928 John P. Clum published the first half of a two-part article that signaled an important shift in Western Apache historiography.[1] In the essay titled simply "Es-kin-in-zin," Clum fashioned a life history of the legendary Western Apache leader *haské bahnzin* (fig. 3).[2] Clum's article was written with great empathy and a genuine desire to understand past events from the viewpoint of someone whose life was irrevocably altered by the incursion of Euro-Americans into the Apache homelands. Yet, when Clum described the Camp Grant Massacre, one of the most pivotal episodes in *haské bahnzin*'s life, he turned surprisingly to non-Apache sources rather than depicting it from the perspective of his subject. Lamentably, nearly every author who has written on this topic has followed in Clum's footsteps.[3] Of the scores of articles, books, and Web pages that portray the Camp Grant Massacre, practically all recycle the incident from the recollections of the American participants.[4] Curiously, even those expositions sensitive to the Apache experience have tended to rely on these partial and incomplete sources.[5]

The Camp Grant Massacre remains a salient moment for contemporary Western Apache peoples.[6] Although a difficult part of their history, it continues to instruct Apaches and non-Apaches about the sacrifices of those who have gone before and the circumstances that have shaped our modern world. The story of the massacre was first preserved by personal histories and has since been maintained in part through Western Apache oral traditions.[7] Apache narratives enhance our understanding of the massacre, not because they necessarily constitute more factual versions but because they

Figure 3. *haské bahnzin* in 1888.

afford alternative, even complementary, accounts. Oral narratives reinvigorate the stories of the disenfranchised and dispossessed, shedding light on those lives that have long been excluded from this historical record.[8]

Increasingly, scholars have valued the historicity in oral traditions and critiqued the bias of Western-based textual histories.[9] Given that written *and* oral historical accounts are similarly the products of a complex process that entwines the past with the social and political present, theorists have progressively given consideration to how "the data of history and the data of tradition taken together form a congruous and more believable whole."[10] While some fret about the contested nature of the past, other researchers more optimistically embrace the multiplicities of history.[11] Sally Engle Merry, for instance, sanguinely argues that divergences are themselves an avenue for understanding people and the past, for varying accounts are "neither true nor invented but are cultural interpretations of events made within particular historical contexts."[12] This chapter provides the basis to begin understanding the massacre from the perspective of Apache peoples.

To write about the Camp Grant Massacre from Apache viewpoints offers a much more intricate knowledge of the event, spinning new strands in the web of histories as it empowers those voices that have previously been silenced. In this chapter, six Western Apache versions of the Camp Grant Massacre will be considered, not to deduce one "true" account but rather to expand an alternative interpretation of the terrible morning of April 30, 1871, and the events preceding and following it. Although the murder and captivity of Western Apache men, women, and children in this instance does not discount the violence various Apache groups perpetrated throughout the eighteenth and nineteenth centuries, it does help us better apprehend the broader context in which these mutual hostilities occurred.[13] Apaches were not the nomadic brigands represented in dime novels but longtime residents of the Southwest desert who experienced a deep and complex affinity to the landscape that American colonialism radically threatened.[14] The narratives that follow are distinct from non-Indian accounts in the same way that William Kessel discerned in his analyses of Apache oral traditions: "White and Apache accounts differ significantly with regard to specific details and with respect to the interpretation of the meaning of these events."[15] I argue that it is precisely these discrepancies that bring new insight.

Following Jan Vansina's typology, I provide three oral histories ("eyewitness accounts . . . which occurred during the lifetime of the informants") and three oral traditions ("passed from mouth to mouth, for a period beyond the lifetime of the informants").[16] Notably, some Apaches, such as elder Eva Watt, would view these narratives as simply history, in this case meaning true accounts of past events.[17] The oral histories were obtained from the unpublished notebooks of Grenville Goodwin archived at the Arizona State Museum; the oral traditions, from a discontinued magazine, an obituary, and a recent interview. San Carlos Apache elder Jeanette Cassa helped translate and make sense of the texts. These narratives are presented with minimal editing and commentary, without obtrusive mediation of each speaker's telling. This is history through the words of Apache elders—testamonials that encourage contemplation of the Western Apache experience from their own standpoint and consideration of the ways in which history is an experience lived and relived with each telling.

Lahn

In 1948 Richard van Valkenburgh published an oral tradition of the massacre related to him by an Apache man identified only as "Old Lahn."[18] Valkenburgh met Lahn at an acorn-harvest camp near Oracle, Arizona, on the north side of the Santa Catalina Mountains, possibly at *dah nagołgáí* (White Spots Up There), a flat grassy area just north of the small town.[19] Valkenburgh stands out from his contemporaries because he specifically sought out an Apache's viewpoint. It is clear from the publication that Valkenburgh fanned the poetic fire of Lahn's story and possibly even supplemented the tale with his own knowledge of the assault. This is typical, Vansina writes, for "any interview has two authors: the performer and the researcher."[20] Nevertheless, both the core of the story, which is highly consistent with other Apache versions, and the numerous cultural references Valkenburgh could not have found in written documents make it likely that much of this account comes directly from Lahn.

The Apache elder began his story by linking the landscape to the origin of the conflicts between Apache groups and Euro-Americans, subtly illustrating how, as Keith H. Basso writes, the Western Apaches' "sense of place, their sense of their tribal past, and their vibrant sense of themselves are inseparably intertwined."[21] Standing on a rocky knoll just above the town of Mammoth, Lahn said, "My story begins at the base of that shaggy red ridge which drops off toward the river bottom." At this place, the troubles began when Mexicans killed three women of the Aravaipa band called the *tcéjìné* (Dark Rocks People).[22] Peaceful prior to these unprovoked murders, the *tcéjìné* then fled to the hills and planned their revenge, Lahn recounted. The peace treaties Aravaipa and Pinal bands eventually made with Mexicans and Anglo-Americans did little to abate the troubles and violence. Lahn continued:

> Then came a time when Santo and *haské bahnzin* stopped their people from coming down here to the Little Running Water [Aravaipa Creek] to plant crops. For years the Aravaipa lived like hunted beasts in the Santa Teresa and Galiuro ranges. And— against *haské bahnzin's* wishes—some young men did accompany the Pinal on raids, lest they starve.
>
> Then came news that there was a new white *nant'an* [headman] at Camp Grant. It was four moons before the chiefs agreed to ask for peace. *Haské bahnzin* won because he said, "It makes no difference where we die. I'd rather we be killed down by the Little Running Water than have death sit beside us here in the mountains!" With suspicion deep in their hearts the Aravaipa sent five old women, one of whom was *haské bahnzin's* mother to Camp Grant to ask for peace. The old women were treated kindly. In two days they returned with the news that the *nant'an* would hold council . . . at the rising of the fourth sun.
>
> . . . On the rising of the fourth sun, Santo, *haské bahnzin* and the sub-chiefs walked into Camp Grant. After a long *yoshidii*, or council, it was agreed that the Aravaipa would surrender their weapons and be placed under the protection of [Lieutenant] Whitman and his soldiers. When they had finished, *haské bahnzin* laid a large rock on the ground before the *nant'an* and said: "We have faith in you. You have spoken to us like men and not dogs. I shall bring my people to you. And so long as this stone shall last the Aravaipa Apache will keep peace with the Americans."
>
> Smoke signals puffed into the sky. In a few days over 500 Aravaipa straggled in from the mountains. After surrendering their weapons and placing their names on the census roll, the *nant'an*

told them that they could return here to their old homes by the Little Running Water. Then came the day when the *nant'an* called *haské bahnzin* to Camp Grant and said, "Your people have been home for two months and have kept the peace. They have worked hard and their crops are growing. In two suns from now, which will be the white man's first of May, we will have a fiesta and barbecue."

But even with this good news *haské bahnzin*'s heart was heavy. María Jilda Grijalva, his good friend and the *nant'an*'s interpreter, had whispered bad news into his ear. Just a few days before, some Pinal Apache who had passed through the Aravaipa camp, had raided and killed an American near Mission San Xavier. The young people, unaware of the bad news, began to dance—right on this flat that spreads before us. As the voices of the singers echoed up and down the canyon the Aravaipa, young and old, came to watch the dancers as they moved back and forth in the glow of great fires. *Haské bahnzin* was still uneasy at the news from Santa Cruz and did not join the dancers. Going through the crowd he tried to make the watchers return to their camps, on those high bluffs above us, and be alert. But believing that they were protected by the *nant'an* at the nearby fort they paid no attention.

Only when the moon had passed across the southern sky to drop into the west did the exhausted dancers lie down on the ground and go to sleep—the men on this side and the women on the other as was custom. Slowly the fires burned down, flickered and then died in the darkness that follows the moon. From out of the east came the first light of Blue Dawn Boy. Not a leaf fluttered in the mesquite. Then way down the canyon there was the warning twitter of the vermilion flycatcher. Creeping through the shadows toward this place were the *sáikìné*, or Sand House People, whom the Americans call the Papago. Silently they crept up the bluff—over the very trail we just climbed. . . . Moving swiftly with their mesquite war clubs loosened they surrounded the sleeping dancers. Striking in every direction they began to smash the skulls of the sleeping Aravaipa.

The screams of the dying ripped open the clear morning air. Roused from his sleep, *haské bahnzin* ran from his *kowa* or wickiup, toward the dance ground. And as he yelled for his warriors to stand and fight, a Papago club crushed his head. Crumbling, he fell to the ground amidst the slaughtered bodies of his people.

After finishing those on the dance ground the Papago began to hunt out those in the *kowas*. That's why I avoided those stone rings over there—for they are places of death. And from that rim above Americans and Mexicans shot down those who tried to flee up-canyon. Yes! There were Americans from Tucson there. We found out later that they were the ones who planned the whole thing! And when those human wolves with black and white skins got through with their killing they set fire to every *kowa* they could find before starting back toward Tucson. They circled Camp Grant so that the *nant'an* and his soldiers would not know what they had done. They carried into captivity 29 Aravaipa children!

The buzzards were beginning to circle when something stirred under a pile of the dead. Pulling himself loose, *haské bahnzin* tried to shake the dizziness from his bloody head as he staggered across the dance ground toward his *kowa* that stood under the cottonwoods which we passed before starting to climb the bluff. His *kowa* had not been burned. But before him on the ground lay the bodies of his young wives and their five children! Then from under a bundle of grass he heard the whimper of a baby. Bending over he pulled back the grass and picked up his only living child—the tiny Chita!

With the baby in his arms he avoided the dance ground and followed the rims until he reached that high point which noses so sharply down into the canyon. Turning back to look down on the scene of the massacre of the Little Running Water, *haské bahnzin*, the last of the Aravaipa chiefs, breathed a curse of vengeance against all white men!

Sherman Curley

On March 12, 1932, Grenville Goodwin interviewed Sherman Curley, otherwise known as *m-ba-lse-ślā*.[23] Curley, like his mother, was of the *tcéjìné* band, a group with a long history in the San Pedro Valley and Aravaipa Canyon.[24] He was born around 1855 and died at age eighty-two.[25] This is an oral history, the story of the massacre as Curley, a survivor, recalled it sixty-one years later. The themes and details that emerge in Curley's chronicle correspond with other narratives and the documentary record, including the relocation of the camp eastward four to five miles prior to the carnage, the dance that led warriors to relax their guard, and the mutilation of women and children. Curley's account is important because it illustrates the humanity of the victims, the panic of the battle, and the horror of witnessing one's family and friends killed.

Bob Macintosh's father and his wife went down to *tu-dn-tl-ij-sikun* [Blue Water Pool, Camp Grant]. They stayed there two days, and then came back and told about it. They brought some big sacks of tobacco back with them. The new Indian agent had given them those. The agent had told this man when he went back to tell all the Apaches living in the mountains nearby, to gather together, and come down and camp near the agency on Aravaipa Creek. The Apaches were still wild then. About one day after this man got back with the tobacco, they had gathered together, and the whole band moved down, and made their camp on Aravaipa Creek, about four miles above the agency. In those days there was lots more Apaches than there are now. They stayed at this camp on the Aravaipa for four or five months. They used to gather all kinds of wild fruit on the mountains, and they gathered *tl-o-na-di-tise* [wild hay], and took it down to the agency, and to Camp Grant to sell.

Now some men said that they would give a dance to celebrate their coming into the agency. The dance was to be tomorrow night, and notice was sent out to the different camps along both sides of the Aravaipa. They started in the next evening to give their *tl-e-gû-chi-taśl* [night dance]. They danced all through the night and almost till sunrise.

There was a big ridge above their camps, and one on the other side too. During the night a big bunch of Mexicans and Papagoes had got up on these ridges, and surrounded the camp completely. The Mexicans and Papagoes . . . fired on them while they were still dancing. They killed a lot of people this way. They all scattered. The scouts and soldiers down at Camp Grant didn't know what was going on. I ran into an arroyo. I had my bow and arrows, and I pointed at them as if I was going to shoot. This scared some Mexicans and Papagoes back, who were after me. I ran on, trying to get away, but four of them followed me, but they did not kill or hit me. In those days we Apaches could run fast, but we cannot do this now. I ran in behind some rocks, below an overhanging bluff finally, and hid there. They shot at me, but could not hit me, those four enemies. They four were afraid to come close. I shot arrows at them. Finally they ran away, and left me. I ran on up the side of the mountain, to the top, and stayed there. Some others who had gotten away were on top of this mountain also. It is called *m-ba-ma-guśl-î-he* [place and translation unknown]. The sun was getting really low now. We stayed on top of this mountain all night. The next day one man went back to the place where we had been dancing. He found lots of dead Apaches there.

Some of the women and girls who had long, nice hair, they had cut a round place right out of the scalp, leaving the hair on, and taken it away with them. I don't know why they did this. This man came back, and told about it.

Next day, the people who had gotten away, and were hidden in different places over the mountains, started to call one another together. When they had all gathered, they sent that same man who had been back to the dance ground and 15 others, down towards Camp Grant. When they were near the camp, they stopped, and rested on some level ground. Then their two head-men, Captain Chiquito and *haské bahnzin*, went and talked with the agent, telling him all that had happened (fig. 4). The agent said he didn't know that this massacre had taken place at all. The officer said that those Mexicans and Papagoes would never come back, and that even if they did, the soldiers there at Camp Grant would know about it first. The officer said that up till this time they had been good friends, and had gotten along all right. This was why he had sent out for them to come in and talk. He sent me up to bury the dead for the Apaches, and he gave out rations to those who had survived. He told them to come back, and settle down again. The band did so, and made their camp on the Aravaipa River, about one mile from the soldiers, so that they would be near them, and have protection.

Figure 4. Chiquito and his wife in 1876.

Walter Hooke

In June 1932 Goodwin interviewed Walter Hooke, *hosh-ke-nes-tz-oot*, and recorded his experiences of the massacre as a young boy.[26] Like Sherman Curley, Hooke was born into the *tcéjiné* band, but like his mother, he was of the *tsédè sgàidn* (Horizontally White Rock People) clan, a group that first settled near Prescott but long ago migrated southward, becoming concentrated in the Pinal and Aravaipa bands.[27] Hooke's account does not dwell on the massacre itself but offers instead an important sketch of where people traveled and what they did before and after the massacre (fig. 5). This chronicle turns on the use of places and place-names, an important element in Western Apache traditional histories.[28] "Sensing places," Basso writes, "men and women become sharply aware of the complex attachments that link them to features of the physical world."[29] Consequently, Hooke's account not only offers an alternative chain of events but also, in its use of place, provides an altogether different way of understanding history.

I was born near *t-îs-cho-o-des-ch-il* [Mescal Canyon], about 70 years ago I think. I heard later that there was no agency at San Pedro when I was born. Later on, when I was about four years old, we all moved to *sai-daśl-kai* [White Sand Up There] there down the river a ways from where Coolidge Dam now is. From this place some of our people went to San Pedro. We had heard that an agency had been set up then. At *na-dah-cho-das-un* [Mescal Big Resting] was *haské bahnzin*, the chief. He and some others went down to see this agent at San Pedro who wanted all our people to come in to his agency. When they came back from there, they brought a big sack of tobacco that the agent had given them.

Now after this some of the people went in to San Pedro agency, and from day to day more and more of us went in. Our family moved to *gash-tla-a-cho-o-a* [Big Sycamore Stands There], and then on to *tûśl-tso-ha-des-lin* [Yellow Water Flowing Down]. From this last place, we went straight on to the agency, *tu-dn-tl-ij-sikun* [Blue Water Pool].

At the agency they gave us rations of flour, coffee, sugar, meat, and corn. We lived by there for two or three years, moving up into Aravaipa Canyon, above the agency, from *gash-tla-a-cho-o-a* [Big Sycamore Stands There] clear up to *tseśl-chî-nadn-t-î* [Red Rock Point So That You See Alone In The Distance].

When I was older we moved to *tse-da-iz-kun* [Rock With Flat Top], right at *gush-tlish-ha-des-jî* [Dark Mud Up There]. At this place there were lots of us. It was during this time that the

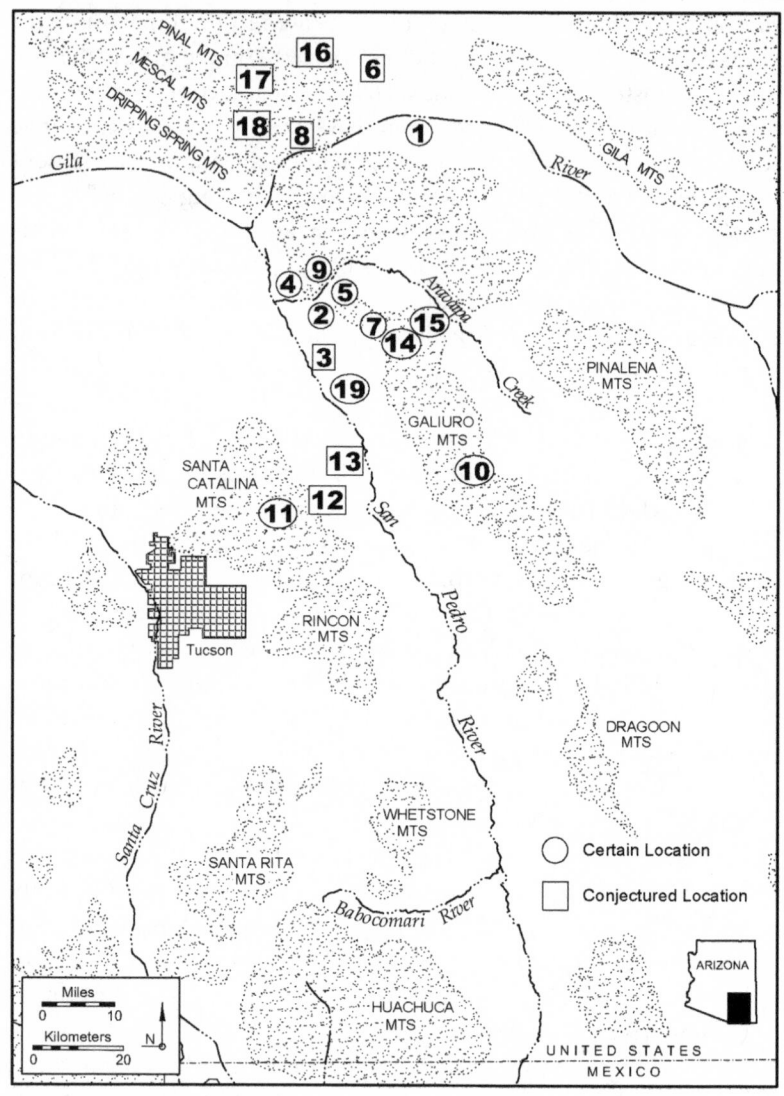

Figure 5. Places Walter Hooke traveled to before and after the massacre at Camp Grant.

No.[a]	Name from Goodwin's notes	Name from place-name project	Translation	Location
1	sai-daśl-kai	sai dałgaí	White Sand Up There	downriver from Coolidge Dam
2	gash-tla-a-cho-o-a	gashdla'á cho o'aa	Big Sycamore Stands There	near the massacre site, on Aravaipa Creek
3	tûśl-tso-ha-des-lin	túłtsog hadaslin	Yellow Water Flowing Down	near the San Pedro River[b]
4	tu-dn-tl-ij-sikun	túdotł'ish sikán	Blue Water Pool	Old Camp Grant
5	gash-tla-a-cho-o-a	gashdla'á cho o'aa	Big Sycamore Stands There	near the massacre site, on Aravaipa Creek
6	tseśl-chî-nadn-t-î	tseł chí nadnt'i'	Red Rock Point So That You See Alone In The Distance	by the Pinal Mountains[b]
7	tse-da-iz-kun	tse da'iskán	Rock With Flat Top	Table Mountain near Aravaipa Canyon
8[c]	gush-tlish-ha-des-jî	goshtł'ish hadesjįį	Dark Mud Up There	by the Pinal Mountains[b]
9	qi-das-il-kai	kįh datsil gai	A White House Up There	Old Painted Cave Ruin, above Aravaipa Creek
10	ziśl-na-zen-yîs	dził naząąyú	Mountain Sits Here and There	Bassett Peak in the Galiuro Mountains
11	ya-ga-si-un	idagé sian	Sits Up There	Mount Lemmon in the Santa Catalina Mountains
12	î-che-jî-ā-a	tsezhį ha'áh	Pumice Rock Up There	near the Santa Catalina Mountains, to the east[b]
13	gash-tla-biśl-na-gal-kai	gashdla'á biłnágolgáí	White With Sycamores	on the San Pedro River[b]

continued

No.[a]	Name from Goodwin's notes	Name from place-name project	Translation	Location
14	tse-da-iz-kun	tse da'iskán	Rock With Flat Top	Table Mountain near Aravaipa Canyon
15	gash-tla-tse-e-chî	gashdla'á tsé hechí	Sycamores Going Out Red	east foot of Table Mountain
16	gash-tla-chî	gashdla'á edichi	Sycamores Meet	by the Pinal Mountains[b]
17	gush-tlish-ha-des-jî	goshtł'ish hadesjįį	Dark Mud Up There	by the Pinal Mountains[b]
18	teśl-chî-nadn-t-î	teeł chî' nadnt'i	Reddened Cattail Alone In The Distance	by the Pinal Mountains[b]
19	iya-nas-pas-si-kasī	iyah nasbạs sikaad	Mesquite Circle In A Clump	the San Pedro Agency, near Mammoth

[a]Numbers represent the order in which Walter Hooke visited the places.
[b]This location is conjectured on map.
[c]The Camp Grant Massacre occurred while Hooke was at this place.

Pimas came and attacked our people, in their camps above the agency. The Pimas killed lots of men, women, and children, more than 100, all up the canyon. One man who got away from there, came to where we were living and told us about it. Now all of our people gathered together at *qi-das-il-kai* [A White House Up There]. From here some of them fled to the Pinal Mountains. Our bunch moved to *ziśl-na-zen-yîs* [Mountain Sits Here and There], and from there to *ya-ga-si-un* [Sits Up There]. We lived at *ya-ga-si-un* [Sits Up there] for quite a while, and then moved to *î-che-jî-ā-a* [Pumice Rock Up There] and lived there for a while. We had no horses then, but had to pack everything on our backs. For this reason we would have to stop and rest for a couple of days at every spring. The next place we went to was *gash-tla-biśl-na-gal-kai* [White With Sycamores], where we stayed for about one month. From here we went to *tse-da-iz-kun* [Rock With Flat Top], right above *gash-tla-tse-e-chî* [Sycamores Going Out Red].

While we were at this last place we heard that our chief, called *da-nash-chî* had been back into the agency, and talked with the agent. The agent told him he wanted him to look for all the other people and find where they were living. So *da-nash-chî* set out riding a mule, to try and find us all. He went to *na-da-des-das-un* [possibly Mescal Grows Thickly], and tracked us down to *ya-ga-si-un* [Sits Up There], and looked for us on the top of this mountain, all over he looked. Finally he found us at *gash-tla-chî* [Sycamores Meet]. He got there about mid-afternoon, and at our camp talked to us, telling us that the agent said for him to send back all the people he could find to the San Pedro agency. That mule he was riding died, but he had another mule to ride back. We will go back in two days he said. So in two days we all started out for the San Pedro agency again. We camped at *gush-tlish-ha-des-jî* [Dark Mud Up There], and at that place heard that some of our people had already been in to the agency and drawn rations. So we moved back below *teśl-chî-nadn-t-î* [Reddened Cattail Alone In The Distance], the same place where the fight with the Pimas had been. From here we went down to the agency, at *iya-nas-pas-si-kasī* [Mesquite Circle In A Clump], and drew rations.

bija gush kaiyé

Goodwin recorded the following interview with *bija gush kaiyé* in June 1932.[30] She was of the Pinal band and married to a headman, although it is unclear which one. An oral history provided from a woman's viewpoint, this interview is unique and focuses notably more on rations, food, and survival strategies, such as cutting hay to sell to the soldiers at Camp Grant. *Bija gush kaiyé*, it seems, escaped the massacre because, on the eve of the bloodshed, she traveled some distance from the camp on the Aravaipa to attend a medicine ceremony (fig. 6). She claimed that about one thousand Apaches were killed, surely not a literal estimate but one meant to suggest an almost unthinkable number of murders.

Now my husband and *haské bahnzin* and that White man—he was an agent of some kind—talked over being friends together at *tu-dn-tl-ij-sikun* [Blue Water Pool]. That White man said he wanted to treat our people well. He gave out no rations though.

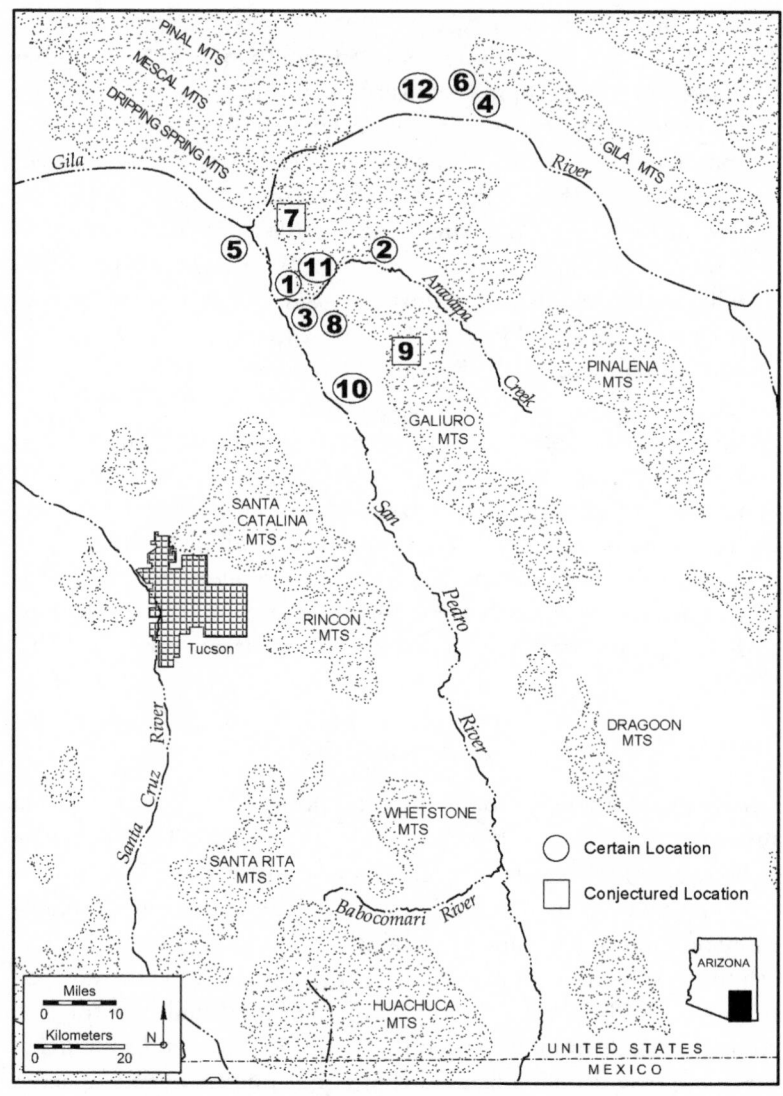

Figure 6. Places *bija gush kaiyé* traveled to before and
after the massacre at Camp Grant.

No.[a]	Name from Goodwin's notes	Name from place-name project	Translation	Location
1	tu-dn-tl-ij-sikun	túdotł'ish sikán	Blue Water Pool	Old Camp Grant
2	tse-na-di-tin	tsé yinaditin	Rocky Crossing	in Aravaipa Canyon
3	tu-dn-tl-ij-sikun	túdotł'ish sikán	Blue Water Pool	Old Camp Grant
4	tsesl-tsut-da-des-dzuc	tseł tsug dades dzuk	Yellow Rocks Coming Down Jagged	southeast of (new) San Carlos
5	nadn-lit-choh	nadnlid cho	Big Sunflower Hill	Malpais Hill, on the San Pedro River
6	tsesl-tsut-da-des-dzuc	tseł tsug dades dzuk	Yellow Rocks Coming Down Jagged	southeast of (new) San Carlos
7	ha-ke-da-dzil-kai	hakida dził kai	Come Up The Mountain	near the San Pedro River[b]
8[c]	gash-tla-a-cho-o-a	gashdla'á cho o'aa	Big Sycamore Stands There	near the massacre site, on Aravaipa Creek
9	—	—	—	"Away, up on the mountains"[b]
10	iya-nas-pas-si-kasī	iyah nasbạs sikaad	Mesquite Circle In A Clump	San Pedro Agency (near Mammoth)
11	qi-das-il-kai	kịh datsil gai	A White House Up There	Old Painted Cave Ruin, above Aravaipa Creek
12	—	—	—	Old San Carlos

[a]Numbers represent the order in which *bija gush kaiyé* visited the places.
[b]The exact location is conjectured on map.
[c]The massacre occurred while *bija gush kaiyé* was at this place.

Now the five of us started back to *tse-na-di-tin* [Rocky Crossing]. *Haské bahnzin* had two or three wives at that time.

After a while *haské bahnzin* came back to our camp and said to my husband, "Let's go down and see the White people again at *tu-dn-tl-ij-sikun* [Blue Water Pool] and make good friends with them this time. I will take my wife that was down there before, and you take this—your wife" (me). "All right," my husband said. So the four of us went down there again to *tu-dn-tl-ij-sikun* [Blue Water Pool]. There were lots of soldiers there. When we got there my husband and *haské bahnzin* talked with the White men and made good friends with them. The agent there they talked with. Now it was fixed so there would be no more trouble between us and the White people.

Then we went back home and separated: *haské bahnzin* and his wife going to *gosh-tla-a-na-chi* [place and translation unknown], and we going back to *tsesl-tsut-da-des-dzuc* [Yellow Rocks Coming Down Jagged] in the Gila River canyon. We stayed there a long time and then heard there were lots of Indians living down close to *tu-dn-tl-ij-sikun* [Blue Water Pool] and drawing rations there. So we went down there again and camped at *nadn-lit-choh* [Big Sunflower Hill] where the rations were being issued. That was the first time I ever saw flour, sugar, or coffee. After we got rations, we moved away again this way to *tsesl-tsut-da-des-dzuc* [Yellow Rocks Coming Down Jagged]. Two other camps moved back with us. We had lots of rations, flour, sugar, coffee, meat. We had no bags to put them in, so had to dump all into our burden baskets. They gave us corn also. Later on we went back for rations again, and this time when we moved away a lot of people came with us. We camped at *ha-ke-da-dzil-kai* [Come Up The Mountain]. Later we went back to *gash-tla-a-cho-o-a* [Big Sycamore Stands There], near *tu-dn-tl-ij-sikun* [Blue Water Pool]. Some *sli-na-ba-ja* [Some Who Hunt on the Horse, a White Mountain Apache band] had heard that there were rations being given over here, and so had come over also.

Now we lived close to San Pedro. The women used to go out and cut hay and sell it to the soldiers for their horses. For this, they would get a red ticket on which they could draw rations or get calico and other things. While we were there, the uncle of my husband got sick in our camp. So my husband said, "Let's take him about a mile down the valley and sing over him there at the camp of a big medicine man called *ni-ba-bi-je-yi.*" So they did, and down there they sang over him all night, till almost dawn.

Just about dawn, some Mexican men came out over a hill above our camps. Now we heard a shot. Then there were lots of Mexicans, *sáikìné* [Tohono O'odham], and Americans all round us. They started to shoot into us. Men, women, and children they killed. They must have killed about one thousand of us, I guess. Only a few of us got away, up on the mountains. Later on the agent at San Pedro said that the people who had attacked us didn't belong to him and he never told them to do this. So those who were left of us went back down to San Pedro again and started drawing rations again and made friends again with the White people there. It was *chu-gero* who had come out to our different camps to tell us to come in again. We went to *iya-nas-pas-si-kasī* [Mesquite Circle In A Clump], and big rations were issued to us there. There were lots of soldiers also. We all camped at *qi-das-il-kai* [A White House Up There], up high, because we were scared of being attacked again. The women started again to cut hay, and sell it to the soldiers. *Nantan-bi-tane-kaidn* was down there now. He gave out red tickets to the women who brought in hay, and told them to buy burros with them, so they could pack the hay in on the burro instead of on their backs. . . .

Now the agent said we would all move to San Carlos and that he wanted all the Indians to come to that place. So we came on over the mountains in a big bunch and got to San Carlos. The White men with their teams and wagons had to go way round by Bowie, and up to Fort Thomas, and then down the river to where we were.

Sally Ewing Dosela

The next narrative is an oral tradition told by Sally Ewing Dosela to Paul R. Machula before her death on Christmas Day in 1996.[31] This account is brief but powerful, a difficult story for her to tell, according to Machula, for she "obviously felt deeply the horrible injustice her family had experienced." Yet, Dosela also asserted that this story reflects the profound connections her people made and continue to make to their homeland, while it testifies to the survival of a people who have suffered great inequities. As Machula observed, "Mrs. Dosela was not just 'telling me a story' that day. In her quiet, respectful way she was teaching me a powerful lesson . . . that life is sacred. It is holy and beautiful. It should not be taken because of hatred. As human beings we are prone to sometimes ugly passions. Tragically, at times we become victims of those passions."

> Men from Tucson killed many people, some of them members of my family, at *al waipa* [Camp Grant]. . . . The sister of Uzbah was there. She was visiting her aunt. The people wanted to have a "sing," and so almost all the men had left their families to hunt for meat in the mountains. About four in the morning Uzbah's sister heard some people come into the camp. She believed they were bringing water into the camp. But, "Why so many?" she thought.
>
> Then, she heard the guns. She also heard the people start crying, and the children began howling. It went on a long time. Uzbah's sister ran away from there. She found a horse. She held on to that horse with one of her legs over its neck, so she couldn't be seen. Then, she went up a trail into a hollow area [a box canyon on Aravaipa Creek]. She hid there. Later she came down and found her cousins and aunt lying all around. All were dead. Blankets were wrapped around the people, and they buried them there.

Jeanette Cassa

One early morning in February 2002, Jeanette Cassa spoke about the Apache experience in the Aravaipa area to T. J. Ferguson, Vernelda Grant, and me. Recited in English, the narrative was recorded by shorthand in a notebook and later reviewed by Cassa. She had lived along the San Pedro for a time in the 1950s but learned most of the story from elders and those of her generation whose grandparents actually suffered the direct violence of the massacre. Also, her father-in-law Ed Cassa was "descended from the Aravaipa band and hailed from the same *tsé binest'i'é* clan as *haské bahnzin*."[32] As far as she knew, the Apache name for the confluence of the San Pedro River and Aravaipa Creek was *łednłii* (Flows Together), and Camp Grant used to sit just north of this spot. After a pause, Cassa began to talk softly but steadily about the massacre. Her version, like Sally Ewing Dosela's, is more compact and concise than the accounts recorded by Goodwin in the 1930s, a process of compression that Vansina argues is to be expected, for group accounts are "constantly and slowly reshaped and streamlined."[33] Still, numerous features of this story correspond with other versions, such as the advance warning, the dance, the use of war clubs, and the taking of captives. Cassa's recital illustrates continuity through oral tradition and the way in which events of long ago continue to have deep meaning today.

> As the men from Tucson were coming, an Apache scout saw them heading towards Camp Grant. He found a little Apache boy and told him to run back to where the Apache were camped near Camp Grant and warn them to run away. The boy did so, but when he told the people, they did not believe him because he was so young and so stayed where they were. That night [April 29, 1871], however, a medicine man had a dream, a vision, about what was going to happen. He warned the people and told them to gather near some cliffs where they were camped. They had gathered for a dance to celebrate something. Some stayed and danced, while others left for the safety of the mountains. After the dance by the cliffs on the floodplain, the people just collapsed where they were. The next morning, the events happened. Manuel Jackson saw his mother get knocked down with a piece of wood and killed. He hid in the branches of a wickiup. It was the Anglos and Papagos who did this, but afterwards the Mexicans came and took children and women—and anyone else alive—captive.

A Fusion of Narratives

These Western Apache narratives converge and diverge in interesting and important ways. Several compelling congruencies concerning details can be found, such as the listing of rations (flour, sugar, coffee, meat, and corn) by both Walter Hooke and *bija gush kaiyé*,[34] and the reference to gathering hay in the narratives of *bija gush kaiyé* and Sherman Curley.[35] Several important correspondences are also seen between the oral histories and the later oral traditions, such as

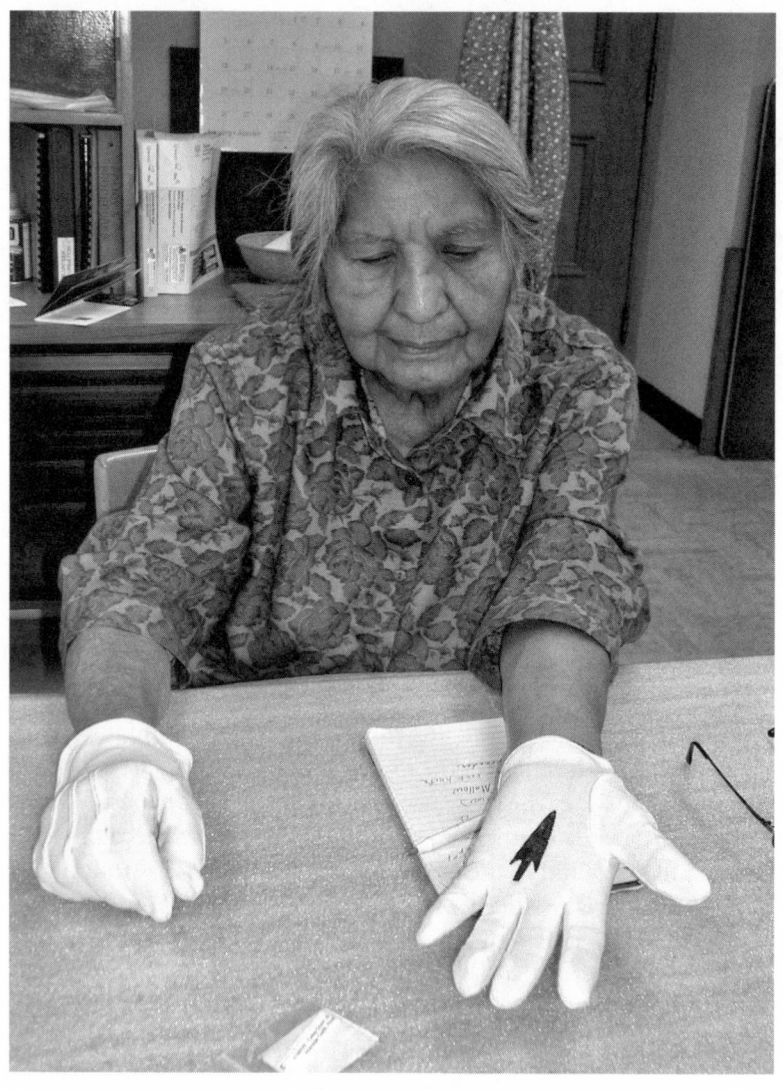

Figure 7. San Carlos Apache elder Jeanette Cassa holding a
metal arrow point made in the Apache style, archaeologically
recovered from Camp Grant.

celebrating the night before the massacre (discussed by Lahn, Curley, Cassa, and Dosela) and fleeing into the mountains after the attack (discussed by Curley, Hooke, *bija gush kaiyé*, and Dosela).[36] The celebration is a recurrent focus of more-recent narratives shared by other Apache elders. Adella Swift learned of the massacre from her grandfather Andrew Noline, a survivor who saw his mother murdered and his sister abducted. As Swift recounted, "They had a feast. The women were cooking all day. They all got together and had a little dance."[37] Dickson Dewey's grandfather similarly reported: "He said he was lucky to get away. They were having some kind of all-night dance. All night, 'til daybreak."[38] Elder Wallace Johnson observed in 1990, "They don't expect anything. I don't know why those guys turn against the Indians. The Army had given them food to use at the dance."[39] And Norbert Pechulie heard from his mother, "They had had a big dance, a big celebration, the night before."[40]

Also significant is how almost all the narrators weave geography through their stories, structuring events around specific locales. Collectively, these narratives provide a structural convergence, painting a picture of the massacre that involves several key narrative landmarks: the move close to Camp Grant and the following celebration at this new location, the attack at Big Sycamore Stands There, and the ensuing flight deep into the sanctuary of the mountains.

Several isolated divergences parallel these convergences. For example, Lahn and Jeanette Cassa were the only storytellers to include an unheeded warning of the attack, an element of foreshadowing. Another variation, although slight, is the time of the attack: "during the night" (Curley), "about four in the morning" (Dosela), "just about dawn" (*bija gush kaiyé*), "first light" (Lahn), and "morning" (Cassa). Such minor discrepancies could have numerous causes, including faulty memories, evolving narrative plots, varied contexts in which the stories were related, or simply differing experiences of the original witnesses.[41] The last possibility seems a reasonable explanation for many of the minute inconsistencies, especially given that close to five hundred Apaches were in the vicinity of Camp Grant at the time of the massacre.[42] Surely, each person's experience differed to some degree, giving rise not to a single oral history but an array. Walter Hooke, for instance, may not have told Goodwin about the warning simply because his family was not at Big Sycamore Stands

There at the time of the attack. No solitary experience or story can fully capture the intricacies of an event like the Camp Grant Massacre.

Stories from the Apache viewpoint that oblige us to rethink the event from new angles do not so much detract from as expand on previous writings. Apache narratives round out a one-sided story, making this history more complex but also more realistic. The effect of these Apache narratives is particularly pronounced when we juxtapose their general patterns with some of the central themes invariably highlighted in the current literature. In the extant corpus, nearly every account begins with an investigation of sundry depredations committed by Apaches in the months before the massacre. For some observers, these raids and murders of non-Apaches serve as explicit justification for the "retaliation" perpetrated against the dozens of sleeping Apache families at Camp Grant.[43] Others underscore the injustice of the attack, however, by suggesting that different Apache bands that had not yet surrendered to the government had committed these crimes.[44] Whatever the merit of these arguments, it is striking that such discussions are lacking in the Western Apache accounts (with the exception of a brief mention in Lahn's chronicle). The Apache narratives tacitly refute assertions of Western Apache links to the raids. The absence of discussion suggests that the Western Apaches were unaware that these raids, for which they could be blamed, had occurred and consequently had little notion why they were attacked. At least, this is what the narrative silence, perhaps even purposely, would lead us to believe.

As will be seen in chapter 3, another motif stressed in the non-Apache literature is the meeting of the attacking party at the Rillito River. At a prearranged spot, Tohono O'odham, Mexican American, and Anglo-American combatants met, obtained provisions, and selected a leader. Many narratives emphasize the number of the participants, highlighting the larger proportion of Tohono O'odham and Mexican American participants. These accounts do not mention that while this group was preparing for war, the Apaches were preparing for a celebration. Accordingly, readers of most published texts feel the story swelling to a crescendo the day before the massacre, whereas the audience for the Apache stories shares the relative calm of a settled and peaceful people getting ready to feast. The double treachery of being attacked during a time of celebration and peace is not adequately conveyed in the current literature.

Reports of the attack itself are similarly one-sided in Anglo-American texts that describe how the Anglo-Americans and Mexican Americans sat on a nearby hill shooting at fleeing Apaches while the Tohono O'odham did the sordid work of battering women and children with mesquite clubs. Only in the accounts authored years later, long after the passing of the actual attackers, do we hear of the rape of young girls, which, like the clubbings, are consistently attributed to the Tohono O'odham.[45] In accounts like those of Sherman Curley, however, we do see hints of a greater culpability on the part of the entire attacking party, as we also learn of the distress Apaches felt upon receiving news about the brutal treatment of their loved ones.

Most writers in the published literature end their tales with the trial in Tucson that charged 100 men with the murder of 108 Apaches, accounts that conclude dramatically with the verdict of "not guilty."[46] Yet, in the Apache versions, the trial is not even mentioned. If survivors of the massacre were even aware of the tribunal, they either considered it an inadequate vehicle of retribution or recognized it for the judicial farce that it was. For the Western Apache people who called the San Pedro River and Aravaipa Creek home, the massacre was just one episode in a larger saga concerning not just the loss of life one spring morning but also the loss of land—indeed, the loss of an entire way of life. Thus the Apache narratives, rather than finishing with an unequivocal verdict or conclusion, remain ambiguous and uncertain. The massacre does not constitute an isolated story but an unfolding and as yet unfinished tale that connects people to their ancestors. These Apache stories, experienced firsthand and then retold through the generations, remind us that history is multivocal, multifaceted, and a vital part of who we are today.

3

COLLECTIVE HISTORIES

Just ten years after the massacre at Camp Grant, Helen Hunt Jackson published *A Century of Dishonor*, a scathing critique of the American government's treatment of Native Americans. Surveying the unjust wars, violated treaties, and flawed policies that afflicted Indians since America's founding, Jackson argued that the history of the American government "convicts us, as a nation, not only of having outraged the principles of justice ... [but also] of having laid ourselves open to the accusation of both cruelty and perfidy."[1] Jackson offered as evidence the tragic histories of seven tribes, including several firsthand accounts of massacres. Among these is "Massacres of Apaches," which concentrates on the Camp Grant Massacre, citing verbatim the disturbing 1871 reports of Lieutenant Royal E. Whitman and Dr. Conant B. Briesly, the post surgeon.

More than 120 years after the publication of *A Century of Dishonor*, Larry McMurtry's *Oh What a Slaughter* appeared, a very different recounting of various massacres in the American West during the 1800s. Whereas Jackson, a social activist who was appealing, she said, "to the heart and the conscience of the American people," opposed the government's treatment of Native Americans, McMurtry acts as little more than an apologist, defending the use of force and violence.[2] Of the Sacramento River Massacre in 1846, for example, in which upward of 175 California Indians were killed, McMurtry claims, "in fairness" to the attackers, that "the *general* threat from Indians was real."[3] Thus the murder of these particular Indians, was understandable if not excusable, even though they were perfectly innocent. McMurtry also considers the Camp Grant Massacre, providing a standard account that begins in the spring of 1871 and continues to General Crook's martial expeditions.

Jackson's account of the Camp Grant Massacre intends to expose the injustice of American practices; McMurtry's depiction seeks to justify frontier violence and demonstrate its inevitability. Yet, significantly, both authors employ exclusively Anglo-American sources. Consequently, although more than a century separates these authors, and they draw different morals from the story, they tell similar tales. This continued reliance on Anglo texts is not altogether surprising, given that army reports and newspaper articles documented the events as they unfolded. While undeniably critical to our understanding of what transpired at Camp Grant, through the decades these texts have been imbued with disproportionate force and authority, as if they provide the *only* story. Meanwhile, Apache narratives, long marginalized and silenced in the mainstream, continue to be recounted among Apaches today and have also been recorded as texts, as the previous chapter illustrates.

To many, a historical account is like an heirloom—a gold watch or a precious antique vase—whose fate and integrity are not assured as it passes through the generations. An heirloom may be carefully protected and remain intact, or it may be lost, stolen, or broken. But a story or history is neither tangible nor concrete in obvious ways, for the materials of its construction are past experiences viewed and interpreted through distinctive cultural and perceptual lenses. This construction is evident in Apache narratives that draw on an oral tradition, structure themselves around local places and placenames, and invert the mainstream, stereotypical role of Apaches from raiders to guardians. Still, Apache narratives are not fabricated from thin air. They do not represent individual flights of fancy but arise from and reveal actual events, places, and personalities. They exhibit convergences with non-Apache sources and each other.

To assert that a narrative of the past has a social component and exhibits historicity is to say that it is both perpetually remade and timeless.[4] But this is only a contradiction if one insists that historical claims must be either objective or subjective, when the line between the two is rarely so clear. Most would agree that the Camp Grant Massacre transpired on April 30, 1871, and yet even recognizing such a basic fact requires cultural knowledge of the Gregorian calendar and a cultural value that emphasizes absolute over relative time—an emphasis not often seen in the Apache narratives, which typically recount, "We went to place X, it happened, and then we went to place Z." Historical accounts are made in the crucible of fact and fiction, forged in the space between objective and subjective experience. Thus instead of thinking about historical accounts as an heirloom, an object, I prefer to think of history as a form of remembrance, a kind of *trace*.[5] The term *trace* in this sense has two related meanings—that which is left behind, a vestige; and that route which is followed, a path. Remembrances result directly from preceding events and thus present historicity; they also are avenues that lead us to the past, a process that involves social engagement. Traces are *representations* and therefore require interpretation, making the question one of translation, of decoding and unraveling the twisted cultural, historical, and political skeins of narratives.

In this chapter, I seek to examine an array of histories, the traces of the past, to understand how the massacre unfolded, its causes and consequences. The idea of traces is a useful point of departure because it conceptually links the present with the past, recognizing the possibility of historicity in narratives as well as the social milieu in which accounts are made and remade. Drawing on multiple remembrances and texts implements an approach of multivocality, a comparative method in which the whole is constructed expressly through polyphony. The result is collective not in the sense that remembrances are unified but that multiplicity creates a collective of histories that transcends the conventional version told from *A Century of Dishonor* to *Oh What a Slaughter* and nearly every text in between. Ultimately, this approach allows us to see the massacre from the perspectives of both victims and perpetrators, from the intersection of individual agency and structures of power, and as an event that neither began nor ended in 1871.

We Are Surrounded by Four Sacred Peaks

More than three hundred years ago, the San Pedro Valley was already a contested space, as suggested by the first detailed map of southern Arizona, drawn by the Jesuit missionary Father Eusebio Kino in 1695. Along the San Pedro River are more than a dozen villages represented in this image by simple circles and named Qui-buri, Oacoa, and Muihibai, for example. These were the homes of the people known to the Spaniards as Sobaipuris, an ancestral group of the Tohono O'odham. Just east of the waterway is a label in bold capi-tal letters "APACHERIA," a region populated by the Jocome, Jano, and Suma peoples. These groups, we now know, were proto-Apachean communities, loosely allied for raiding and war, and united through shared linguistic and cultural practices.[6]

When Kino first visited the Sobaipuri village of Quiburi in 1697, one of the first sights he witnessed was a dance of Sobaipuri war-riors around poles topped with Apache scalps.[7] Kino was not dis-pleased to happen upon the scene because the Spanish authorities needed the Sobaipuri as auxiliaries to stop, or at least slow, raiding by Apache groups farther south toward Sonora and west toward Tucson. The Sobaipuri, in turn, seemingly desired an alliance with the Spaniards for access to new resources such as cattle and to learn of the foreign religion they preached. The result was a growing con-flict cultivated by colonial designs that pitted Apache groups against the alignment of the Sobaipuri and the Spanish. Within a century of Kino's arrival, however, the Sobaipuri had left their villages along the San Pedro River to join their kin near Tucson. The efforts of the Spanish military to fill the resulting void in the San Pedro Val-ley were spectacularly unsuccessful,[8] and by the late 1700s Apache groups were deeply anchored in the valley. Free from Spanish au-thority, they lived by raiding, hunting feral cattle and horses, and planting corn and beans.[9] "It was evident that the Apaches had per-fected a way of life which called for no increase in their own terri-tory and no desire to defeat the Spaniards in what the latter called battles," Edward Spicer once wrote. "The Apache aimed merely at supplying their shifting camps in the mountains of southeastern Arizona and southwestern New Mexico by raids whenever they wished on the settlements of Spaniards, Opatas, and Pimas."[10] But this "perfected way of life" was far from perfect, for it depended in part on a violence that deprived innocent people of their livelihood and intensified an enmity that fueled colonial aggression. Apache raiding and warfare, however warranted as self-preservation or self-defense, perpetuated a mood of brutality that infused the Southwest for generations.

The Spanish documents provide a glimpse into Apache lifeways centuries ago but do not offer decisive evidence for how long Apache peoples have made their home in what is now southeastern Arizona. Apaches who trace their own origins through the genesis of clans, as well as traditional band territories, suggest that the connection to Arizona is ancient indeed.[11] Two Apache clans, the *dáhàgòtsùdń* and the *ságùné*, are said to have emerged far to the south in the San Pedro Valley and to have begun traveling northward centuries ago (fig. 8).[12] Traditional band territories also suggest a long and deep affinity with the San Pedro Valley. Named for a place called *tséìjìn* (Dark Rocks) in Aravaipa Canyon, the Aravaipa band called the *tcéjìné* (Dark Rocks People) have the strongest attachment to the San Pedro Valley. Related to the Pinal band, the Aravaipa band possibly split off after both groups, seeking a new place to plant crops and harvest agave, immigrated from the north. The Pinal band called *'tìs'évàn* (named for *'tìsévà*, or Cottonwoods In Gray Wedge Shape) lived just north of the Aravaipa Apaches in the now aptly named Pinal Mountains.[13] Although the San Pedro Valley is the traditional homeland of the Aravaipa band, other Apache groups, such as White Mountain bands and the Chiricahua Apache, depended on the luxuriant river valley.[14]

The connection to place, the vibrant bond between Apaches and the land, begins with the birth of the Apache people. Ramon Riley, a White Mountain Apache tribal member, explained in an interview that the Apache creation story tells of how the people emerged from the center of four sacred mountains: "Our creation story tells us we are surrounded by four peaks—the sacred mountains. In the east is black, Mount Baldy; in the south is turquoise; in the west is red, Four Peaks; in the north is white, San Francisco Peaks. Some people say the south mountain is Mount Graham but my mother always told me they were the Sierra Madre in Mexico."[15] The San Pedro Valley is encompassed by these summits, which are integral to the local landscape and are woven into the larger Apache cultural fabric. "There are songs from time immemorial about these mountains," Riley added.

By the late 1700s, with the Spanish having a tenuous hold on the frontier in Sonora and the Sobaipuri having no permanent settlements, Apache groups reigned over the San Pedro Valley. Historians have written that this period was relatively calm, due in part to

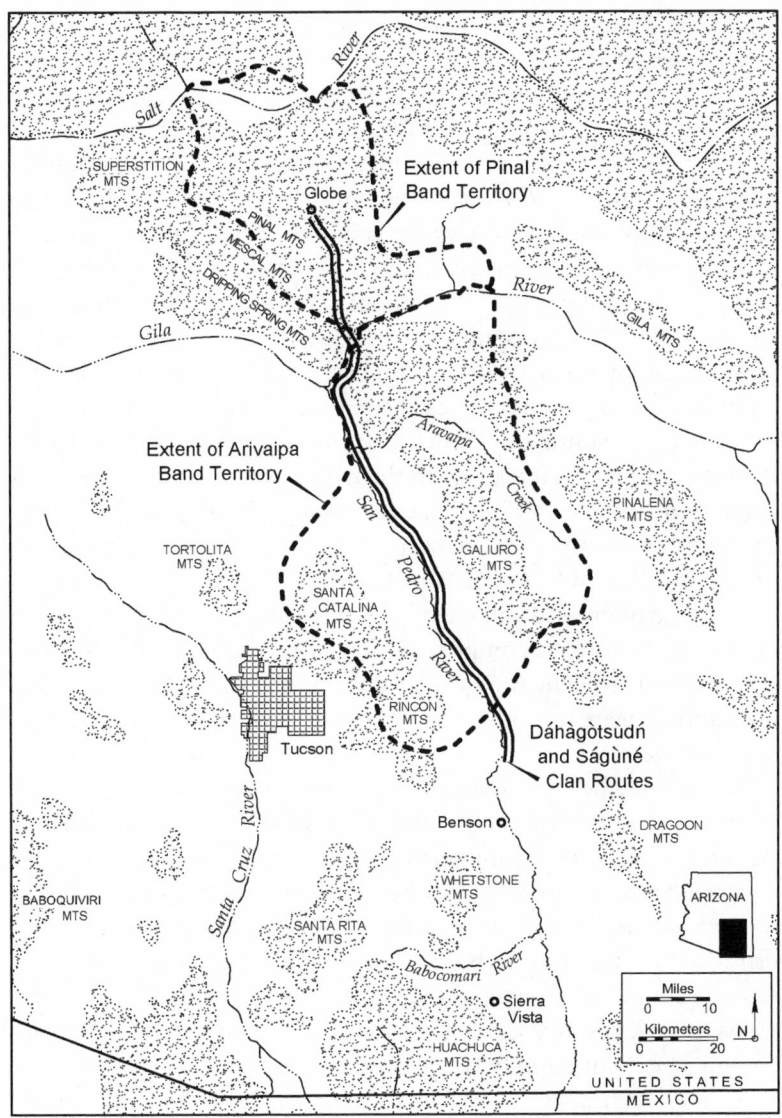

Figure 8. Apache clan migrations through the San Pedro Valley and Arivaipa and Pinal band territories circa 1850.

a Spanish policy of "trade and presents" that aimed to make Indians "so completely dependent on the Spanish trader that their very lives would be in his hands, both economically and defensively."[16] Apaches were given guns of poor quality that constantly needed new parts and repairs and were offered herds so that they might be less tempted to raid. Yet during this time Apaches, too, sought armistices. For instance, a group of Aravaipa Apaches came to Tucson in January 1793 to sign a peace treaty.[17] But even as the Spanish made overtures toward peace, they conducted hostile military operations. In 1793, several months after the treaty with the Aravaipa Apaches was signed, Spanish troops from Tucson left on a campaign for Aravaipa Creek, eventually capturing and beheading two men, a woman, and a young boy.[18] As the Spanish government maintained its policy of northern expansion through force, Apache groups continued, in turn, to raid settlements throughout the borderlands.[19] Even with the birth of Mexico in 1821, little changed. In 1832 a force of 200 soldiers and civilians attacked Apaches in Aravaipa Canyon. "After a relentless and valiant attack that lasted all of four hours, our citizens proclaimed a complete victory," one Mexican witness wrote. "Seventy-one Apache warriors lay dead on the field. Thirteen underage captives were taken. Two hundred and sixteen horses and mules were recovered."[20]

Many Apache narratives point to the violence they suffered at the site of cultural contact, challenging those histories that portray Apaches simply as warmongers. Apache elder Lahn, for example, suggested that the real troubles began when Mexicans arrived from Sonora and murdered three Aravaipa Apache women whose only crime was concealing where some Pinal Apaches were living.[21] Consequently, the Aravaipa Apaches left their ripening crops in the fields to seek revenge against the Mexicans. Lahn's story articulates the Apache distinction between raiding and warfare. In the Apache language, raiding is literally translated as "to search out enemy property," whereas warfare is translated as "to take death from an enemy."[22] In 1836 Apaches also sought peace when fourteen leaders arrived in Tucson, declaring that they were there "for the sole purpose of seeking a stable and enduring peace."[23] The Mexican soldiers and a company of Apache men agreed to ten points, including ending violence and repatriating captives. The Apaches agreed for the time being to "settle at the juncture of the Aravaipa arroyo and the San Pedro River" at a place known as *lednłįį* (Flows Together), the heartland of the Aravaipa band and soon to be the location of a military installation called Camp Grant.

Will the Indians Take the Country?

In the years immediately following the Gadsden Purchase of 1854, when the San Pedro Valley first came under the authority of the U.S. government, it remained in the hands of Apache peoples.[24] Still, American pioneers entered southern Arizona in search of land for ranching and farming, stands of timber, and undiscovered ore. Establishing lines of transport and communication was an important step toward colonization, and several roads that crossed the San Pedro were built, including the Southern Emigrant Route (1846), the Birch Mail Line (1857), Leach's Wagon Road (1857), and the Butterfield Overland Trail (1858).[25] During these early years, some Apache groups accepted the presence of Americans, while others rejected the latest interlopers in their territory.[26] As raiding increased, the U.S. government decided that "military posts should be established directly in Apache country, where punishment could be prompt and effective."[27] On May 8, 1860, Company B of the 8th Infantry officially erected Fort Aravaypa at the confluence of the San Pedro River and Aravaipa Creek.[28]

Within a year of its founding, Fort Aravaypa, whose name was changed to Fort Breckinridge, was deserted altogether when Confederate troops entered Arizona in 1861.[29] Union soldiers returned to the San Pedro River in the spring of 1862, briefly occupying the outpost and rechristening it Fort Stanford to honor the governor of California. During the Civil War, American civil and military authorities were consumed with the country's fratricidal conflict, which consequently gave Apaches greater sovereignty. With the reconciliation between North and South, however, an increasing number of Americans headed west, and the military had more resources to focus on the "Indian Problem."[30] In the fall of 1865, the outpost on the San Pedro River—now dubbed Camp Grant after Ulysses S. Grant—was revived and housed soldiers charged with controlling the Apache population. The garrison consisted of a parade ground,

Figure 9. Camp Grant in 1871, with the guard house and adjutant's office to the right and the commandant's quarters, officers' quarters, and officers' mess in the distance beyond the parade ground.

blacksmith shop, photo lab, and several dozen adobe buildings, tents, and brush structures, which did not weather well (fig. 9).[31] An 1870 report of the conditions at Camp Grant described the buildings as leaky, rotted, and "totally unfit for quarters."[32] The soldiers' health was also constantly strained: in 1869, at any given time over 35 percent of the men were sick from malaria, dysentery, catarrhal infections, and other illnesses.[33] Bemoaning the "sickness, heat, bad water, flies, sand-storms and utter isolation," Captain John G. Bourke famously called the installation where he was stationed "the most thoroughly god-forsaken post of all those supposed to be included in the annual Congressional appropriations."[34]

While the formal raisons d'être for Camp Grant were to protect mail routes and permit agricultural production in the San Pedro Valley, these responsibilities were fundamentally a mandate to sub-

Table 1. Estimates of Non-Apache and Apache War-Related Deaths, Injuries, and Captures, 1866–1878

Year	Non-Apaches killed	Non-Apaches wounded	Non-Apaches captured	Apaches killed	Apaches wounded	Apaches captured
1866	27	2	0	155	61	41
1867	22	19	0	172	6	43
1868	58	23	2	130	65	49
1869	154	49	0	205	20	41
1870	137	42	2	100	1	31
1871	57	39	2	254	47	44
1872	36	10	0	194	35	21
1873	2	2	0	193	0	84
1874	0	5	0	247	5	293
1875	0	1	0	45	0	137
1876	0	1	0	41	0	33
1877	0	1	0	10	0	14
1878	0	0	0	13	3	25
Total	493	194	6	1,759	243	856

Source: Data compiled by Allison Diehl from territorial-period newspapers.

due Apache populations.[35] Soldiers stationed at Camp Grant not only responded to reports of Apache raids, they actively sought out Apache rancherias to capture and kill Apaches, as well as seize their recoverable property and burn their crops.[36] Although Apaches throughout the 1800s were portrayed as the rampant murderers and abductors, documentary evidence illustrates that Apaches, in fact, suffered disproportionately from these conflicts. According to the records of the U.S. army, the government killed 528 Apaches in southern Arizona between 1866 and 1875, while Apaches killed forty-two soldiers in all—a ratio of nearly thirteen to one.[37] The army did not record statistics for the few U.S. soldiers taken captive, but 340 Apaches were captured during this same period. A study of territorial-period newspapers between 1866 and 1878 by Allison Diehl gives us rough estimates of the numbers involved.[38] We discover that some 1,759 Apaches were killed compared to 493 non-Apaches; and 856 Apaches were taken captive compared to 6 non-Apaches (table 1).

Apache warriors undeniably killed settlers and soldiers and took women and children prisoner. Joseph Hoffman, an Apache from Cibecue who was born around 1847, recalled how Apache men once went to war against the Akimel O'odham in retribution for an earlier attack.[39] The Apache warriors came across an Akimel O'odham camp, surrounded it, and waited patiently until daybreak. While the Akimel O'odham were still asleep, the Apaches attacked with arrows and set fire to the brush houses. The war party returned home with captive children to a dance of victory. "When the Pima children were brought there they were divided among the women whose relatives had been killed," Hoffman explained. "This way these women got all the Pima children in place of the ones who had been killed. This is called *gegodza* [to be paid back], and when it was done they felt all right." Western Apaches also engaged in raiding throughout the borderlands, which they often organized when stored meat was low and hunger seemed imminent.[40]

These raids were far from inconsequential for the victims, who often experienced genuine anger, fear, and loss. Americans afflicted by raiding became ever more vocal, linking their own fate with that of the wild new U.S. territory. In the late 1850s, Tucson was a small town, as one visitor recalled with no great affection, describing the 600 or so inhabitants as an assortment of "horse-thieves, gamblers, murderers, vagrants, and villains."[41] Historical archaeologists have observed that Tucson began to take on a more formal character in 1862, when William Oury compiled the first property records, and in 1872, when the town was chartered and Mayor Sidney DeLong sold property on behalf of the city to interested buyers.[42] By 1870 more than 3,000 people lived in Tucson, then Arizona's largest settlement, and the town kept growing and prospering.[43]

Given the rise of Tucson during the 1860s and 1870s, its populace felt that the town and its neighboring regions rightly belonged to them by virtue of their labor, citizenship, and capitalist aspirations. This attitude can be seen in the very first editions of Tucson's fledgling paper, the *Arizona Citizen*, which immediately concerned itself with ridding Arizona of Apache raiders, if not Apaches altogether. Editor John Wasson wrote an 1870 article entitled, without irony, "Will the Indians Take the Country?" which indicates the degree to which Anglo-Americans overlooked their own recent arrival and the fact that Apaches then controlled most of southern Arizona. Wasson wrote that "the citizens are in fear of an attack that will drive them from the country, and which will again turn that rich and productive portion of the Territory over to the savages. . . . what force is there to combat these savages; protect the mail route, and prevent the farmers being driven from the country?"[44] As one scholar has noted, during this period Arizona's newspapers "regularly portrayed Tucson itself as a town under siege, methodically misconstruing sporadic and unrelated Apache raids as a concerted campaign perpetrated by a unified tribal enemy."[45] Not surprisingly, then, in November 1870 the paper was pleased to announce that the governor of Sonora, valuing "the difficulties to be encountered and the sacrifices to be made by the volunteers who are undertaking the campaign against the Apaches," raised the reward to three hundred dollars for each Apache scalp turned over to the government of Mexico.[46]

The Akimel O'odham near Phoenix and the Tohono O'odham west of Tucson were also the frequent targets of Apache raiding and warfare, a cycle of violence that dated back to at least the 1600s. O'odham warriors accompanied each successive force of Euro-Americans on military expeditions into the San Pedro Valley to attack Apache villages. The O'odham had several motives for participating in these missions east of their ever-shrinking territory, including a continued alliance with Euro-Americans, retribution for Apache raids, and monetary rewards. (At one time O'odham were paid a hundred dollars per Apache killed and ten dollars per woman or child captured.)[47] Stories about Apache incursions into O'odham areas continued to evoke strong emotions even decades after the cessation of hostilities.[48] Sevier Juan, an O'odham elder, spoke of an 1852 Apache attack. Using a calendar stick (a mnemonic device that records important historical events), he sadly related how the Apaches "killed the old men and burned the houses and all the property except such as they wished to take for spoil. They took the women and children and hurried homeward."[49] Given the violence of such attacks, it becomes easier to understand why the O'odham accompanied strikes into Apache territory and why, when the Anglo-Americans and Mexican Americans invited the Tohono O'odham to wage war against Apaches in the spring of 1871, they assented without much deliberation.

No More Trouble

Apache elder *bija gush kaiyé* recalled one day probably in the late 1860s when the Aravaipa leader *haské bahnzin* came to her husband and said, "Let's go down and see the White people again at *tu-dn-tl-ij-sikun* [Blue Water Pool, or Camp Grant] and make good friends with them this time." Her husband agreed, and a small group journeyed to the post. "There were lots of soldiers there," *bija gush kaiyé* recalled. "When we got there my husband and *haské bahnzin* talked with the White men and made good friends with them. The agent there they talked with. Now it was fixed so there would be no more trouble between us and the White people."[50]

This oral history provides another illustration of how Western Apache groups were not simply reacting to the policies or military tactics of colonial powers but actively suing for peace into the late 1860s. Army documents record one notable instance in December 1866 when Brevet Captain Guido Ilges signed a "treaty of peace" with four Apache leaders, including "Skimapah," likely *haské bahnzin*.[51] In a speech during the meeting, one Pinal leader explained that his people wanted peace simply to gather agave and hunt game in the mountains without being harassed. "We are happy," he said, "to be permitted to visit and come back to the spot where we were born and where we played as children." After the Apaches left in peace, however, Ilges's superiors rebuked him for promising Apaches "what neither he, nor the President nor any intermediate official can give."[52] The military, in other words, rescinded the accord.

Five years later, when a group of five elderly Apache women came into Camp Grant, its commander, Lieutenant Royal E. Whitman, was not so naïve as to offer a treaty without license. On February 28, 1871, Whitman wrote a report to his superiors describing how this small group of women had come looking for a child taken near Salt River a year earlier. The women left for several days and then returned with a small party, the head of which indicated through a translator, a Mexican woman who had once been a captive, that they would like to make a lasting peace. The leader claimed to be a Pinal Apache living in the headwaters of the San Carlos River whose band was "anxious to make terms, and come into this post to remain, to put themselves under the protection of the Government in good faith, to plant corn and have their herds in the immediate vicinity of this post." Later that day, several Aravaipa Apaches arrived also wanting peace. Whitman gave them rations of corn, flour, beans, and meat but insisted on speaking about terms only with their chief. "What the result of all this may be I am entirely unable to conjecture," Whitman wrote in his report. "I think it quite possible they may be acting in good faith, in which case I was very careful not to exaggerate the inducements of a life on a reservation. It is also quite possible the movement may be a ruse to obtain temporary relief, in which case I carefully assured them of the vigorous measures to be taken for their extermination should they persist in their hostility to our common government."[53]

By March 3, 1871, more than a hundred Apache men, women, and children were at Camp Grant. Whitman at first made them report to him daily and placed their rancheria in a wooded area along Aravaipa Creek near the post. Within two weeks there were more than three hundred at the rancheria, and on April 1, 455 Apaches were counted during rations. In late March Whitman wrote, "As their number increased, and the weather grew warmer, they asked and obtained permission to move farther up the Aravapa to higher ground and plenty of water opposite to the ground they were proposing to plant and were rationed every third day."[54] As *bija gush kaiyé* recalled, the Apaches moved about five miles east of Camp Grant to *gashdla'á cho o'aa* (Big Sycamore Stands There), a traditional farming site. Apache elder Walter Hooke recalled that "the agency they gave us rations of flour, coffee, sugar, meat, and corn," a list corroborated by army records.[55] These rations were not dispersed entirely out of charity. General George Stoneman, commander of the Department of Arizona, wrote a contemptuous letter on April 9, 1871, about the Apaches at Camp Grant, observing that "what little they planted during the last year has either been destroyed by drought, or by the troops. Mezcal, one of their main sources of supply, is nearly exhausted in the portion of the country where they dare to live." Stoneman explained that the "dictates of humanity and the spirit of [his] instructions" compelled him to issue rations; however, these supplies also served as an important safeguard against rebellion. "Savage, treacherous and cruel as these Indians are," Stoneman wrote, "they still have enough of human nature in their composition to consider them controllable through the medium of their bellies."[56]

Numbers rose at Camp Grant because of the generally peaceful transactions among the surrendered Apaches, army personnel, and local residents. "They were happy and contented, and took every opportunity to show it," Whitman wrote. "They had sent out runners to two other bands which were connected with them by intermarriages, and had received promises from them that they would come in and join them."[57] As previously discussed, *bija gush kaiyé* recalled that the women who lived near Camp Grant would cut hay for horses, for which they received tickets for cloth and other goods. Whitman claimed that "the amount [of hay] furnished by them in about two months was nearly 300,000 pounds."[58] Some local residents were also content with the new arrangement. "The Indians were often at my house," William Hopkins Tonge, an Anglo-American resident on the San Pedro River wrote in a letter to the commissioner of Indian affairs. "It is true they annoyed me, but their intentions toward all of the farmers near the fort appeared to be kindness. They hunted and made us presents of meat. Their women would collect and bake the mescal plant. And whenever they did so, they would make us presents of the mescal. We would generally give them something in return. The men had many of them disposed of their bows and arrows believing that they were perfectly safe under the protection of the flag and soldiers of the army of the U.S."[59]

The Encouragement of Murder

In Tucson, the response to the peace agreement was at first positive. In an article in the *Arizona Citizen* titled "Peace Agreement by the Pinals—Delightful Hopes Expressed," the author suggested that the Apaches were well treated and that even more bands were being called into Camp Grant.[60] The tone quickly changed, however, when several raids and murders, presumably by Apaches, took place in southern Arizona in late March and early April. For example, a wife and husband were killed in Tubac, and cattle were stolen at San Xavier. The fury of Tucsonans peaked in mid-April 1871 when a group of Apaches killed Alex McKinsey on the San Pedro River. A party of Anglos pursued the attackers, but more than a hundred

Apache warriors confronted them and killed three men.[61] Then, the following morning, a mail carrier was attacked near San Pedro Crossing. The genuine anger and frustration of Anglo-Americans is apparent in an *Arizona Citizen* article titled "Encouragement of Murder." Published on April 15, 1871, it contradicted its earlier report, stating, "As we declared at the time, the Camp Grant truce was a cruel farce. . . . There is not a reasonable doubt but Camp-Grant-fed Indians made the raid on San Xavier last Monday."[62] The assumption that the Apache raiders were under the protection and support of the American government only amplified the anger of the citizens.

That Apaches under the guise of peace at Camp Grant committed raids in southern Arizona is highly improbable. Yet, the people of Tucson *believed* this charge to be true and drew upon this conviction to motivate and condone their violence. Even if the allegations were true, the raiding activities of a few cannot possibly excuse the outright massacre and enslavement of so many, if guilty at all then only by association. Nevertheless, because the attackers and later writers used these charges to suggest that the victims brought the carnage upon themselves, the claims deserve careful consideration.[63]

As early as 1872 an army officer suggested that the innocence of the Apaches at Camp Grant could be determined by tracking the days of rations and of the raids: "I submit the following: From the time they came in, these Indians were counted and their numbers recorded every three days. I kept no journal at that time, but very frequently went with Lieutenant Whitman and counted the various bands; those counts, of course, were recorded, as the issues were made accordingly, and in the records, I believe, are preserved. Compared, then, the date of any depredation in Southern Arizona, or elsewhere, with the records will show whether or not any of these Indians could have been engaged therein."[64] In the trial that followed the massacre, Whitman himself said, "The Indians called my attention to the fact that at the killing on the San Pedro [they were accused of], they were all in at the Reservation. I found that, at that time there were more Indians at the Reservation than at any other time."[65]

According to multiple military accounts, the Apaches were given rations and systematically counted every three days throughout the entire month of April 1871.[66] Working from two known dates of rationing (April 4 and 22), we can deduce that rations were given on April 1, 4, 7, 10, 13, 16, 19, 22, 25, and 28 (fig. 10).[67] Local newspaper accounts recorded the following Apache attacks during this same period: a raid at San Xavier on April 10, an attack by more than a hundred warriors on four citizens along the San Pedro River on April 13, an attack on a mail carrier twelve miles east of San Pedro Crossing on the morning of April 14, and an engagement with Cochise and 150 warriors twelve miles east of San Pedro Crossing on April 16.[68] We know from the military count on April 28 that there were around 128 adult men surrendered at Camp Grant.[69] Thus, if the Apache men at Camp Grant had been involved in the attacks on April 13 and April 16, nearly every man would have been absent from the Apache encampment at Big Sycamore Stands There.

Some might question the coincidence of the three major engagements occurring on the same days as rations (April 10, 13, and 16). Nevertheless, it would have been nearly impossible for so many Apache men to slip away unnoticed when rations were offered and counts taken. To distribute coffee, flour, sugar, corn, and meat to each of the nearly five hundred Apaches present at Camp Grant in early April would have taken hours and would have greatly increased military scrutiny of the community. If the Apaches at Camp Grant were to have engaged in a raid, they most certainly would have had to leave the night of a ration day, say on April 7, arrive at San Xavier on April 8, then return to Camp Grant on the night of April 9 in time for rations and the count on April 10. Events were distinctly inconsistent with this pattern, however. The attacks occurred on the very days rations were distributed. Based on the apparent fact that it took the attackers from Tucson more than twenty-four hours of constant travel to get to the Apache rancheria, it is highly improbable that Apaches could raid at San Xavier on April 10 and be counted and receive rations at Camp Grant on the same day.[70]

The depredations were most likely perpetrated by Chiricahua Apaches who were never recorded at Camp Grant and whom the army likely engaged on April 16 at San Pedro Crossing, the same place the mail was captured on April 14 and not far from the attack on the San Pedro on April 13. Notably, too, less than a month earlier army troops had encountered Chiricahua Apaches, "Cochise's band

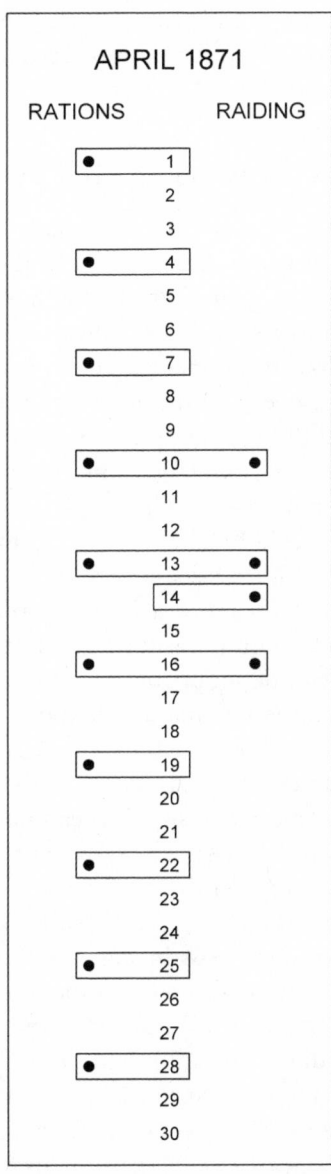

Figure 10. The timing of rationing at Camp Grant and reported raiding in southern Arizona during April 1871.

from 150 to 200 strong," in the nearby Whetstone Mountains.[71] The Western Apaches at Camp Grant almost certainly did not commit the raids used to justify their slaughter.

Blood Flowed Just Like a River Downstream

Throughout the early part of 1871, Tucsonans had been holding a series of public meetings to vent their frustration and anger about Apache depredations. William Oury, a longtime resident of Tucson and former army officer who had fought at the Alamo, later wrote that "many valiant but frothy speeches were pronounced and many determined resolves were resolved," but ultimately no definite action resulted from these meetings.[72] Oury and several other local leaders, Sidney R. DeLong and J. W. Hopkins among them, met with General Stoneman, but he was of little help, simply persuading the delegation that they ought to take care of their own problems. Some weeks later, one night after yet another futile meeting, Oury met Jesús María Elías, who observed acidly, "all your speechifying and resoluting amounts to nothing, and no good can come of it. In the meantime the slaughter of our people goes on."[73] From this sub-rosa meeting was hatched the scheme to ask Tohono O'odham allies to join the Tucsonans and attack the Indians at Camp Grant. Oury was to gather up a group of Anglo-Americans; Elías was to encourage Mexican Americans; and Francisco, the headman of San Xavier, was to recruit Tohono O'odham. All would meet under a veil of secrecy along the Rillito River just north of Tucson.

Tohono O'odham oral traditions, as related to Ruth Underhill in 1933 with a calendar stick, explain that Apaches killed two Mexicans near Tucson in an area known to them as the Hollow Place. When the "pale white Mexicans" learned of the Apache attack, they approached the O'odham and told them that they wanted war and that "they were going to Little Springs, to chase the enemy." Messengers sent out to the O'odham villages of Coyote Sitting and Mulberry Well said to the warriors, "Don't stop for food or for weapons. The women at the Hollow Place will be grinding corn for you and the pale whites will give you guns."[74] According to one O'odham oral tradition, the men sent bundles of sticks to the different villages ten days in advance. One stick was to be thrown away each day to keep track of when to go on the warpath.[75] At seven o'clock on the morning of April 28, 1871, an O'odham messenger arrived at Oury's home and informed him that an O'odham force had gathered at San Xavier "and would leave for the place of rendezvous at the [Rillito Creek] as soon as they had their breakfast."[76] Later that afternoon, around one hundred Tohono O'odham men met some fifty Mexican Americans and six or more Anglo-Americans on the outskirts of Tucson.[77] Some men carried their own weapons, and those without were furnished guns and provisions by Adjutant General of Arizona Samuel Hughes. His wife, Atanacia Santa Cruz Hughes, recalled some years later, "Mr. Hughes did not go to Camp Grant but he furnished the means to go; he approved of the plan and gave the ammunition and the arms."[78] As the men prepared to leave, Elías was elected commander of the party, in part because so few Anglos were present, and by four in the afternoon the company had headed out for the crest of Redington Pass, between the Santa Catalina and Rincon mountains east of Tucson.[79] "Some Mexicans came too," the O'odham calendar stick says referring to Elías and his followers, "and they led the way."[80]

On the following day, April 29, Captain Thomas S. Dunn at Fort Lowell near Tucson discovered the subterfuge and ordered Sergeant Clarke and Private Kennedy to ride without delay to Camp Grant with a written warning. The message from Captain Dunn was terse and to the point: "I am informed that a body of citizens have organized for the purpose of *massacring* all Indians at your post. *You have it*, attend to it." The messengers arrived at Camp Grant several hours after the massacre. Men positioned along the road from Tucson by Oury and Hiram S. Stevens, a Tucson lawyer, likely detained the soldiers for a time, and as Whitman later noted, "the horses that they rode upon were very poor ones, in very poor condition."[81]

While the vigilantes advanced to Camp Grant, the Apaches had little indication that anything was amiss. As noted in chapter 2, multiple Apache narratives even suggest that the group at Big Sycamore Stands There was preparing for a feast to celebrate the new and successful peace.[82] As Norbert Pechulie's mother told him, "They had had a big dance, a big celebration, the night before. They were sleeping. They came upon them."[83] The only indication in the documentary record that the Apaches were celebrating is a brief comment from *haské bahnzin*, who said that he was making "tiswin," a mildly alcoholic drink used for social occasions, when his people were attacked.[84] Other Apache narratives say that the surrendered group was informed of the pending attack, but some did not heed the warning. In one chilling version, Wallace Johnson, an Apache, said, "One guy, who used to live right up here . . . an old man, used to tell me that he was a little boy at the time and he was sent up there to tell the people. 'You going to be killed tonight.' But they didn't believe him."[85] Apache elder Jeanette Cassa said that during the dance a medicine man had a dream about what was to transpire and warned the people who had gathered. Some fled for the mountains, but those who remained were soon caught in the slaughter.

Early in the morning of April 30, some attackers crept along the riverbed with clubs and swords, while men up above on a terrace prepared to shoot at fleeing Apaches with rifles. The carnage began and "blood flowed just like a river downstream," as Pechulie said darkly. *Bija gush kaiyé* escaped the bloodshed because an uncle had become ill the night before, and they took him a mile from the camp to sing over him.[86] At dawn, however, *bija gush kaiyé* recalled hearing gunshots, and then her people came running to the mountains, telling her, "there were lots of Mexicans, *sáikiné* [Tohono O'odham], and Americans all round us. They started to shoot into us. Men, women, and children they killed." Just a boy at the time, Andrew Noline was small enough to hide in the thick bear grass covering his family's *kowa* when the attack began. His mother was hiding with him but ran out to save his infant sister when she was taken by one of the attackers. "His mom went outside and tried to save the baby that was taken away by the Mexicans," Noline's granddaughter recalled. "She tried to get the baby from the horse, and another guy came around and hit her with a club and she fell and never got up."[87] One Anglo-American attacker would later recall, "Naked Indians rushed in all directions, Papago clubs swung, Apaches fell. At that time I was with Bill Oury's Papagos. I stopped some of the Apaches with my saber. That was the only time I had use for a saber, and I made good use of it then."[88] The gruesome details were even remembered years later in Tohono O'odham oral traditions. One elder recalled the violence done to bodies as an expression of hatred: "the men would kill the women, and stood them on their heads in the water

... upside down with arms and legs stuck out at all angles. They sure hated the Apaches."[89] Apaches like Sherman Curley who could fight and run fast enough barely escaped with their lives.[90]

The Apache camp was too far from Camp Grant for the soldiers to hear the tempest of screams and gunfire. The assault lasted less than an hour, and as Oury recalled, by "8 o'clock on the bright April morning of April 30th, 1871 our tired troops were resting on the San Pedro a few miles above the post in the full satisfaction of a job well done."[91] When Lieutenant Royal Whitman received the belated message from Captain Dunn, he immediately sent out two soldiers to bring in the Apaches to the post. The soldiers returned shortly with the news that many Apaches had been killed and the rest had apparently fled. Whitman sent out twenty soldiers and citizens with the post surgeon to help the survivors and to make it understood that they had nothing to do with the violence. Dr. Conant B. Briesly, acting assistant surgeon at Camp Grant, later wrote:

> On my arrival I found that I should have but little use for wagon or medicine; the work had been too thoroughly done. The camp had been fired and the dead bodies of some twenty-one women and children were lying scattered over the ground; those who had been wounded in the first instance, had their brains beaten out with stones. Two of the best-looking squaws were lying in such a position, and from the appearance of the genital organs and of their wounds, there can be no doubt that they were first ravished and then shot dead. Nearly all the dead were muti-lated. One infant of some ten months was shot twice and one leg hacked nearly off.[92]

Sherman Curley recalled that the survivors who were scattered all over the mountains began to call to one another the next day, and they sent down Chiquito, *haské bahnzin*, and a dozen others toward Camp Grant. Whitman supposed that if the Apaches saw him bury-ing the dead, the survivors would understand his good intentions. Whitman's hunch was correct, and he later wrote, "for while at work [burying the dead] many of them came to the spot and indulged in their expressions of grief, too wild and terrible to be described. That evening they began to come in from all directions, singly and in small parties so changed in forty-eight hours as to be hardly recognizable, during which time they had neither eaten nor slept."[93] Dr. Briesly also remembered that Indians began to return the following day when they recognized that the soldiers were innocent of a conspiracy. After speaking with the living and burying the dead, Briesly came to realize his first calculation that some twenty-one Apaches had been killed was wrong: More than a hundred Apaches had been killed, all but eight of whom were women and children. Some thirty more children were missing, taken captive.

The Feeding of the Wolves

While the Tohono O'odham warriors returned to their villages and began a regime of ritual purification, the Mexican American and Anglo-American participants returned to a jubilant Tucson.[94] In the next issue of the *Arizona Citizen*, Wasson began rationalizing the attack in an article titled "Bloody Retaliation," which suggested that the army and the Apache population received fair punishment: "The policy of feeding and supplying hostile Indians with arms and ammunition has brought its bloody fruits. . . . There never was a murder committed in self-defense with stronger provocation or better grounds of legal justification, than in the case under consideration."[95] In the months that followed, Wasson campaigned in defense of the attackers through a series of editorials, as well as testimonials from people who swore that the Apaches murdered at Camp Grant were guilty of various thefts and depredations.[96] Wasson was in part responding to sentiments like those expressed by President Grant, who said that the attack was "purely murder," and General Oliver Otis Howard, who wrote, "under no circumstances whatever can the civilized world justify a deed like this."[97] Wasson tried to discredit Royal Whitman, who was writing letters to various officials and eastern newspapers, as was Conant Briesly, who published a letter in the *Army and Navy Journal*. "I feel no hesitation," Briesly wrote, "in denouncing the whole affair as an insult to the Government, whose honor was pledged for the safety of these people, and a most cowardly and brutal murder."[98]

Convinced that the army would have prevented the attack had they discovered the plot, about three hundred Apaches moved back to Camp Grant, this time nearer to the post. A month later, several army soldiers visiting from another fort shot at *haské bahnzin* when they happened upon him gathering food in Aravaipa Canyon.[99] Some have suggested that *haské bahnzin* was so angered that he went to the home of a friend named Charles McKinney, a 35-year-old Irishman living on the San Pedro River, and killed him out of vengeance.[100] For many years, authors have incorrectly claimed that McKinney was killed in cold blood *before* the massacre, and the author of a recent article even goes so far as to structure the entire narrative of the massacre around McKinney's murder, repeating the chilling statement often attributed to *haské bahnzin*: "I did it to teach my people that there must be no friendship between them and the white man. Anyone can kill an enemy, but it takes a strong man to kill a friend."[101] Although there is no concrete evidence that *haské bahnzin* committed this crime, it was widely believed he did, which only stoked the anger toward Apaches. John P. Clum, a friend of *haské bahnzin*, wrote years later in his defense, "The enemies of Es-kim-in-zin emphasize his crime by saying that the man he killed had be-friended him. They appear to lose sight of the fact that all this treachery, cruelty and murder toward the Apaches was enacted after the most solemn assurances of friendship and protection had been made to the Indians by the commissioned officers of the American Government."[102]

Apache oral histories report that the bands once again returned to the mountains of the San Pedro Valley. *Bija gush kaiyé* recalled that her group went into the mountains after the massacre but eventually came back to the area, staying at *kih datsil gai* (A White House Up There), a cave high up in a remote portion of Aravaipa Canyon, "because we were scared of being attacked again."[103] Walter Hooke recalled that during the summer of 1871 his family traveled to at least six places in the Santa Teresa Mountains, the Galiuro Mountains, the Santa Catalina Mountains, and the Pinal Mountains. "We had no horses then, but had to pack everything on our backs," Hooke remembered. "For this reason we would have to stop and rest for a couple of days at every spring." While at *gashdla'á edichi* (Sycamores Meet) in the Pinal Mountains, an Apache leader spoke with Hooke's band, "telling [them] that the agent said for him to send back all the people he could find to the San Pedro agency."[104]

In September 1871, Vincent Colyer, a peace commissioner sent by President Grant, met with *haské bahnzin*, Chiquito, and other Apache leaders at Camp Grant. At one point Colyer asked the leaders if they would still like to remain in the San Pedro Valley, given all that had transpired there. He wrote, "Answer. The country still pleases them; they wish to remain here; this has always been their home, the home of their fathers."[105] Colyer also visited the massacre site with the Apaches and saw that "some of the skulls of the Indians, with their temple-bones beaten in, lay exposed by the washing of the [creek] and the feeding of the wolves." He caught *haské bahnzin* "wiping tears from his eyes when he saw them."[106] Despite the anger Tucsonans felt toward Colyer and his mission, he succeeded in establishing a reserve for the Apaches that encompassed much of the Aravaipa homeland—the northern reaches of the San Pedro Valley and Aravaipa Creek.

The death of so many family members and friends haunted the Apaches, a suffering intensified by the knowledge that their children were living as captives of the very people who had perpetrated the holocaust. The distress of the Apache community was palpable to the army and other government officials. Whitman wrote that one Apache begged him: "Get them back for us; our little boys will grow up slaves, and our girls, as soon as they are large enough, will be diseased prostitutes to get money for whoever owns them."[107] In the days immediately following the massacre, Lieutenant Whitman and Captain Frank Stanwood tried to retrieve the children, writing insistent letters not only to superiors but also to Reuben A. Wilbur, the Tohono O'odham Indian agent. In one such letter, dated May 17, 1871, Stanwood wrote to Wilbur, "I demand on the part of the United States from you, as agent for the Papagoe Indians, the restoration of the captives. If you think you cannot enforce justice amongst your tribe I will assist you with the troops of my command."[108] By late October 1871, Wilbur had written to Whitman saying that he had learned the fate of eight children.[109] At San Xavier del Bac was one ten-year-old girl who had been shot through the arm. She was in the possession of Jesus Mendosa. Another child was owned by Nicholas Mendosa, and another by José Lucas. In Tucson, Leopoldo Carrillo had custody of one, Manuel Martinez had one, Francisco Romero possessed two captives, and Manuel Duran had sold one six-year-old girl to an unknown buyer (table 2).

Table 2. Captive Children Named in the Documentary Record

Source	Captive	Age	Owner
Wilber Oct. 1871	1	—	Leopoldo Carrillo
Wilber Oct. 1871	girl	6	Manuel Duran (or Duruse)
Wilber Oct. 1871	1	—	José Lucas[a]
Wilber Oct. 1871	1	—	Nicholas Lucas (?)
Wilber Oct. 1871	1	—	Manuel Martinez
Wilber Oct. 1871	girl	10	Jesus Mendos[a]
Wilber Oct. 1871	2	—	Francisco Romero
McCaffrey May 1872	Lola	10	Leopoldo Carrillo
McCaffrey May 1872	Luisa	4	Jose Luis[a]
McCaffrey May 1872	Maria	20 mo.	Nicholas Martinez[a]
McCaffrey May 1872	Juan	5	Manuel Martinez
McCaffrey May 1872	Lucia	3	Francisco Romero
McCaffrey May 1872	Vicente	9	Simon Sanchez
Baptism May 1871	Maria	2	Nicolas Martinez[a]
Baptism July 1871	Dominga	4	
Baptism Nov. 1871	Seferino	0	
Baptism Jan. 1872	Juan	—	Manuel Martinez
Baptism Jan. 1872	Maria Francisca	5	
Baptism Sept. 1872	Maria Antonia	12	Francisco Telles

Sources: Reuben A. Wilbur Collection, file AZ 565, UA; M234, roll 6, Letters Received by the Office of Indian Affairs 1824–1880, Arizona Superintendency 1863–1880, 1872, NARA; St. Augustine Catholic Church Baptisms, MS 296, vol. 3, AHS.
[a]Known to have participated in the Camp Grant Massacre

In May 1872, some of the citizens who wanted to permanently adopt the Apache children retained a lawyer, James E. McCaffrey. In a letter to Richard C. McCormick, the Arizona delegate in Congress, McCaffrey wrote that six children "had been ransomed by some of our citizens, and had been adopted into their families, were living with them, and became much attached to them." The lawyer continued: "Because they (the children) are now Christian and it is an outrage upon Christianity and civilization to force them back into the savage heathenism of the Apaches . . . and because they have no natural guardians, and they desire to [live with] their adopted parents, where they were well cared for, and where [General] Howard knows they were being educated as Christians."[110] These arguments are—to say the least—deceptive. Not only was it illegal to purchase human beings in 1871, but the Americans simply assumed that the children had no biological parents or relatives who could raise the orphans. It is also strange to imagine that the Tucsonans genuinely believed that the parents would want their enslaved children to remain with their captors. The arguments cleverly evade the point that the children were orphaned by some of the people who now owned them and had murdered their families. That these Tucsonans went to such lengths to "adopt" the children and yet maintained such a high-handed stance reflects a time when it was not considered dishonest to claim superiority based on one's civilization and a right of possession based on one's citizenship.

The fate of the other children, perhaps several dozen, is not clear. Andrew Noline, who survived the massacre, continued to look for his stolen sister for years. He became a scout, scouring the countryside of Tucson with his horse, but no trace of her was ever found.[111] Baptism records from St. Augustine Catholic Church in Tucson that list a handful of Apaches may point to the enslaved children. William Tonge wrote on June 8, 1871, that one girl of seven or eight managed to slip away and traveled alone for two days and two nights from Tucson back to Camp Grant.[112] General Howard wrote that two children managed to escape their captors.[113] Hints and whispers of other stories can be found in the documentary record. In 1927 the daughter of Jesús María Elías said that one of the captive children was not Apache but a Mexican girl captured only a week earlier in Mexico.[114] She also suggested that a man named Jimmie Lee, a participant in the massacre, brought back two captives, whom he gave to his sister to raise. Wilbur wrote, "In regard to the whereabouts of the remainder of the captives . . . the remaining 21 were sold into Sonora and sold somewhere in the Altar District."[115] A Tohono O'odham calendar stick recounts a similar end. "The people brought some children back and kept them as their own," it says. "When they were grown, and able to work, they were sold in Sonora for a hundred dollars apiece."[116]

Their Savage Tormentors

As people in the eastern United States reacted to the massacre with horror, local authorities were compelled to press criminal charges. District Attorney Converse W. C. Rowell reluctantly succeeded in this task by leaving a telegram from the attorney general in plain view of the grand jury secretary, Andrew H. Cargill. It read, "If you cannot indict in three days telegraph—we declare martial law and trial by court martial."[117] A court martial would have meant a jury not entirely sympathetic to the murderers. So on October 23, 1871, a United States grand jury found 111 indictments, 108 for murder and three for misdemeanors.[118] With Sidney R. DeLong as the lead defendant, 100 men were charged (table 3). That night Cargill and Rowell were burned in effigy.[119] Rowell remarked several days later, "Public sentiment is very strong in favor of the accused in that section of the Territory, and I have very little hope of convictions."[120] When the trial began in early December, it focused entirely on Apache depredations throughout Arizona history and whether Apaches at Camp Grant were responsible for raids in the months before the massacre.[121] Judge John Titus instructed the jury that they had only to decide if the defendants acted *defensively* or in *malice*—if, in other words, the massacre could be justified. Following a week of testimony and arguments, the jury deliberated for nineteen minutes, came out of their chamber, and acquitted the defendants on all charges.

Some territorial-period residents felt vindicated by the massacre even years later. "Then, and not until then," as one Tucsonan later said, "did 'Uncle Sam' realize it was his bounded duty to prefer the claims of his suffering children to those of their savage tormentors, and hastened to make ample amends for his reprehensible neglect in the much-troubled past."[122] The dramatic verdict provided many writers an obvious point at which to end their tale, but history for Apaches has no such simple finale. For the Western Apache people who called the San Pedro River and Aravaipa Creek home, the massacre was just one episode in a larger saga that concerned the loss of family, vast tracts of land, and an entire way of life.

At about the same time that the jury in Tucson was reading their verdict, Acting Assistant Surgeon Valery Havard, then stationed at Camp Grant, visited the massacre site.[123] There he collected a human skull, brought it back to the fort, and eventually sent it to Dr. Charles McCormick, who then donated it to the Army Medical Museum in Washington, D.C. Directly on the cranium is written "Apache Skull (female) / Arivapa Tribe / Camp Grant, A.T. / Sent by Actg. Asst.

Table 3. A Partial List of Defendants from Surviving Court Records

Andres	Francisco	Miguel
Angel, Juan	Frecon	Miguel, Jose
Antonio, Juan	Fugia	Nicholas
Arisco	Gallego, Ramon	Nicholas
Asedo, Lutario	Gamon	Nunes, Jesus
Asina	Grijalba, Antonio	Oisca
Ausik	Ignacio, Jose	Otunica
Bennett, D. A.	Jajot	Oury, William
Bustamente	Jat	Pablo, Juan
Conception	Jesus	Pasar
Caisini	Joait	Pereosa
Canches, Simon	Juan	Pirus
Coca	Juan Pablo	Ramon
Cocomima	Juan, Jose	Ramon
Crisante	Juan, Jose	Reuteria, Lorenso
Cristoval	Juan, Jose 2nd	Ruelas, Francisco
Dedudi	Julio	Soso, Plasedo
DeLong, Sidney R.	Lee, James	Sowa
Diego	Leuis	Sumad
Domingo, Jose	Lucas, Jose Luis	Tatumu
Elias, Jesus	Luiniup	Teclinepa
Elias, Juan	Luis	Telles, Hilario
Espenosa, Isabel	Manuel	Telles, Juaquin
Etchells, C. T.	Manuel, Jose	Telles, Nicholas
Eugenio	Manuel, Juan	Toaha
Fico	Martin	Tutiwa, Amas
Fieva	Martinez, Nicholas	Viejo, Paseno
Francisco	Mascuna	Ygnacio, Jose
Francisco	Miguel	

Sources: Extract from Day Book of the U.S. District Court, First Judicial District, Territory of Arizona, March 5, 1866–April 16, 1874, Indians of North America—Apaches—Camp Grant Massacre Ephemera File, AHS; Records of the U.S. Commissioner Relating to *U.S. v. Sidney R. Delong*, 1871, NARA-PR.

Surg. V. Havard, USA / December 15th 1871 / From the ground of the massacre of April 30th 1871." It is possible that Havard collected the skull from the surface, as both Colyer in September 1871 and Howard in June 1872 reported seeing bones on the ground. Whitman wrote, however, that his men buried the victims, and a recent analysis by the Smithsonian's Repatriation Office notes that "the condition and color of the bone suggest a subsoil burial." The skull is the remains of a young adult female, perhaps twenty to thirty-four years old. The Smithsonian report concludes: "These remains are Apache, given the direct association with a documented historic massacre, and evidence presented by the collector that the remains were recovered at the location of the massacre within eight months of the atrocity. The physical condition of the remains [is] consistent with the known events of the massacre and the aftermath, indicating partial, or short term, burial and incomplete physical deterioration. Archival and historical records identify the victims of this massacre as members of the Arivaipa band, many of those descendants live on the San Carlos Reservation." The remains were transferred from the Army Medical Museum to the Smithsonian around 1900.

A year after the massacre, in the spring of 1872, General Howard held a "peace conference" at Camp Grant with, amazingly, people who had been sworn enemies only days before, including Chiquito, *haské bahnzin*, Whitman, General George Crook, Arizona governor Anson P. K. Safford, Elías, Oury, Carrillo, Hughes, and Wilbur, as well as a dozen Apache leaders, forty-two Akimel O'odham, and fifteen Tohono O'odham, including Francisco of San Xavier. Lasting several days, the talks focused on reconciling the factions and, because of Apache insistence, repatriating the captive children. This meeting produced several steps toward peace, including the return of six children from Tucson households, an agreement on all sides to refrain from violence, and the establishment of a new reservation for Apaches along the San Carlos and Gila Rivers.[124] *Haské bahnzin* expressed interest in shifting the reservation headquarters "to a place where there was a good water supply, fertile farm land, and a healthier climate, and where they would be farther removed from hostile citizens."[125] Walter Hooke told Goodwin that *haské bahnzin* "wanted for us all to move over to San Carlos, along with the soldiers, where there was lots of water, at the junction of the San Carlos and Gila Rivers. 'That would be a better place for an agency,' he said."[126] The reservation at San Carlos was soon established, and *haské bahnzin*'s people moved there in February 1873.

It is clear, however, that Apaches did not intend to abandon their territories along the San Pedro River and Aravaipa Creek with this move northward. When life became too unstable for *haské bahnzin* at San Carlos, he left for the San Pedro River in 1877, saying, "I will go down to the Rio San Pedro and take some land where no one lives now, and I will make a ditch to bring water to irrigate that land. I will make a home there for myself and my family and we will live like the other ranchers do."[127] *Haské bahnzin* and his family started a new farm at *nadnlid cho* (Big Sunflower Hill), where the modern town of Dudleyville now sits. *Haské bahnzin's* veritable success is suggested in surviving documents, such as an 1879 article reporting that he "is a model rancher; he has taken out a good ditch, has fine herds, and is a good neighbor."[128] An 1881 article claimed that *haské bahnzin* had become an American citizen and reported that "he has a boy 5 or 6 years old and when he dies he wants the boy to have his ranch. He lost all his older children, who were murdered by the Papago Indians on the reservation several years ago. He lives within a half mile of where his children were killed and buried, and when he dies he wants to be buried there."[129] Shortly after he established his home, three or four additional Apache families joined him, also building houses and fences while cultivating the land.[130] An 1885 map of the farm shows a small Apache settlement replete with houses, cornfields, and pastures (fig. 11).

Despite such prosperity—some say because of it—*haské bahnzin* and his Apache neighbors were soon forced off the land. In 1887, after an Indian agent warned *haské bahnzin* that 150 armed citizens were coming to kill him, he fled.[131] "They took 513 sacks of corn, wheat and barley, destroyed 523 pumpkins and took away 32 head of cattle," he later said, calculating his losses.[132] The land was illegally taken, because in July 1885 the Department of the Interior and the Department of Indian Affairs agreed that *haské bahnzin's* homestead was lawfully held.[133] After his escape, *haské bahnzin* was asked if he might return to the San Pedro. "I would not be safe there," he replied, "and would feel like a man sitting on a chair with some one scratching the sand out from under the legs."[134]

I Love My Land Here

Almost as soon as the San Carlos Reservation was established, non-Indians began to trespass upon it.[135] Long before the reservation was created, military authorities recognized that mineral extraction by private interests would maximize Indian displacement with

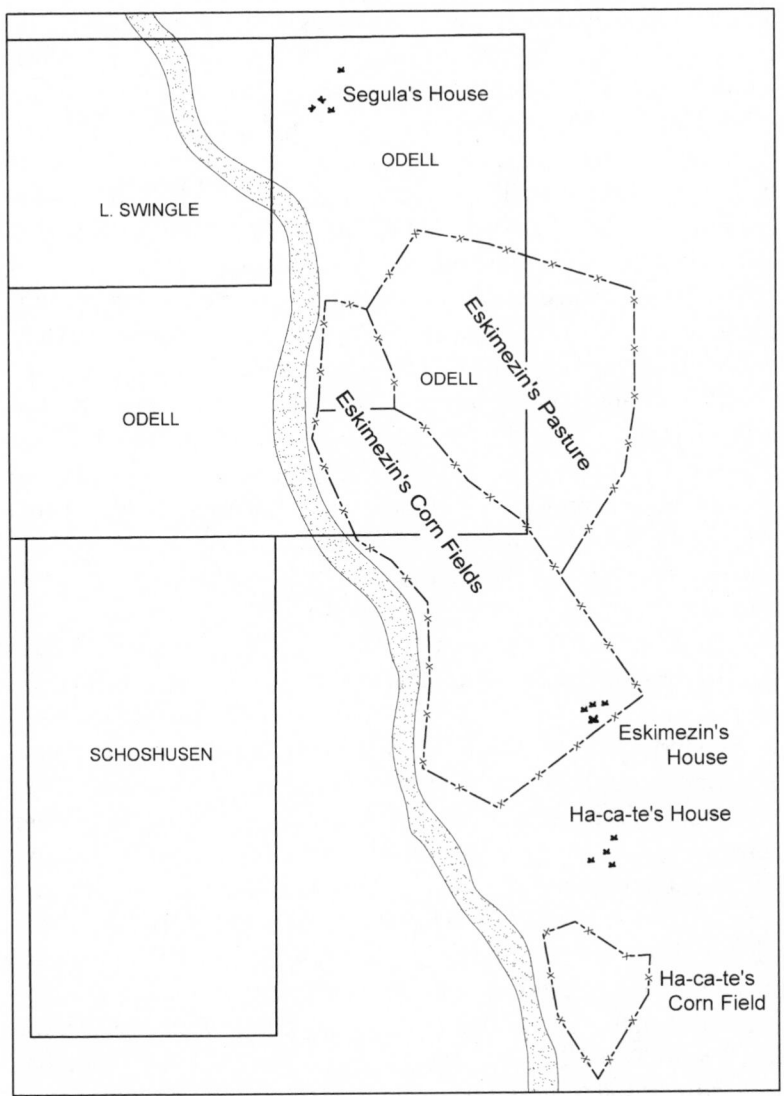

Figure 11. Detail of an 1885 map of the Dudleyville area with Apache farms and land claims of American farmers overlaid.

minimal government resources. Although this program was not purposefully enacted in the San Pedro Valley, Colonel John Green wrote as early as 1870 that "if that section [where Pinal Apaches reside] is as rich in mineral as is supposed, and the people find it out, there will be such a rush, the Indians will be ousted in a very short time, and but little military aid will be required."[136] Exactly a decade later, the San Carlos Indian agent, Joseph C. Tiffany, urged his superiors to clearly define the reservation's boundaries because so "many are interested in trespassing on the reservation on account of the minerals."[137] The next year Tiffany reported that prospectors found prized coal deposits, which were in truth within the reservation.[138] (Notably, Tiffany himself was accused of tricking Apaches into selling him land with coal deposits at a low price.)[139] In 1896 a government inspector produced an agreement that conceded more than 200,000 acres of the southern reservation lands, a region embracing the San Pedro River and Aravaipa Creek, for mineral development. In return the tribe was to receive fair financial compensation.[140]

At one public hearing about whether to relinquish the land, Chiquito reportedly "spoke of his great love for these lands and opposed the agreement."[141] The decision was not left, however, to the Aravaipa band who traditionally lived in this area but to all adult male Apaches then residing at San Carlos, including Yavapai and White Mountain Apaches. Eventually, the measure passed, with 56 percent agreeing to turn over the area known as the Mineral Strip. The land was eventually ceded to several dozen ranchers and farmers, and appropriated for some government projects (table 4). Yet, of the thousands of acres ceded, almost none was put toward mining, and "from the time of the 1896 agreement until 1931, the Apache received $12,433—somewhat less than a dime per person per year."[142] The San Carlos Tribal Council passed a resolution seeking compensation in 1939 and a resolution asking for the land to be returned in 1958. After years of controversy, 232,320 acres of the Mineral Strip were ultimately given back to the tribe in the 1960s and 1970s.[143] The non-Apaches who were living there then, though in some measure innocent of duplicity, were forced to leave.[144]

Although the San Carlos Reservation continued to shrink throughout the early 1900s, Apaches still traveled southward to the

Table 4. Major Land Grants from the Mineral Strip after 1896

Recipient or grantee	Approximate number of acres	Justification
Alder, Elbert	2,880	ceded
Bowman, Huston	9,600	ceded and patented
Bundrick	24,320	ceded and patented
Clairidge, Bros.	1,280	ceded
Cluff, Mary	6,720	ceded
Flieger	1,600	patented
Gomez	7,680	ceded and patented
Hinton, Huston and Jack	7,040	ceded and patented
Hinton, Jack	5,440	ceded
Hinton, Willie	3,840	ceded
House and Bowman	2,880	ceded
House, Urban	2,240	ceded
Layton, Roy	22,400	ceded and patented
Layton, Roy and Glenn	12,800	ceded and patented
Lee Estate, M.	640	ceded
Lee, Ted	320	ceded and patented
Miller, Dave	6,720	ceded
Sanford	2,880	ceded
Smith	4,160	ceded
Smith and Reese	8,960	ceded
Smith, Keith, and Bur McBride	20,480	ceded
Smith, Max and Keith	30,080	ceded and patented
Upshaw	21,120	ceded
Weaver, Bryan	1,920	ceded
—	640	San Carlos Irrigation Project
—	3,200	withdrawn for power sites
—	11,200	embraced in national forest

Source: File 4332 S315 G43, AHF.

Galiuro Mountains, Aravaipa Creek, and San Pedro River. Chiquito and his descendents remained on Aravaipa Creek despite the encroachment of settlers.[145] As early as 1872, Chiquito told an agent he "wished now to come in and be allowed to plant in the valley of the Aravapa Creek."[146] A decade later, an army officer reported that Chiquito and his wives had done just that, living in several small camps along the Aravaipa, growing corn, beans, onions, red peppers, watermelons, muskmelons, cabbage, pumpkins, tomatoes, and potatoes.[147] Still, the lingering fear of Indians and the threat of land and water theft did not dissipate.

Surviving documents report a heated dispute between Chiquito and an African American man, David Waldon.[148] The testimony of a local farmer named Ernie Keilberg on Chiquito's behalf illustrates the serious racial frictions that continued to pervade southern Arizona. "This Indian Chicito [*sic*] is a very industrious old Indian. I have been living neighbors with him for 18 years, and have always found him believable," Keilberg wrote in one letter. "I think this Indian is entitled to any patent to this land if not his right is shurly [*sic*] as good as anybody elses. I have a family living here in the canyon and let me say that I will 100 times over rather have old Chicito for a neighbor than have some Negroes." Waldon, for his part, mistakenly claimed that Chiquito had been gone from his Aravaipa home for seven years after being "banished by the government" for joining a renegade named Apache Kid and for the "murder of Augustin Ruiz." In March 1901 Chiquito, through a letter writer, testified to the Indian agent at San Carlos:

> I love my land here at the Arivaipa Canon and wish to live well and happy. I had never done any things wrong since I came here to the Arivaipa County and I never killed no man yet or else not steal any horses or cows yet. I always try to do what is right all I can. Even I never got drunk yet. The color man had wrote a letter to you about name Captain Chiquita. I am Chiquita here. The black man wrote bad letters about me just because the color man wishes to have all my farm. The color man just big liar, that all. That along time ago the bad Indians had killed one Mexican here at the Arivaipa, but that I never did that. I never killed no Mexican or any white man yet. . . . These Indians, they don't belong to San Carlos, they belong to San Pedro County. They never got drunk and they always working, all the time. . . . Everything is going on very nicely here at Arivaipa.

In the documents, Waldon seemed genuinely hurt and implied that neither he nor Chiquito were at fault for the misunderstand-

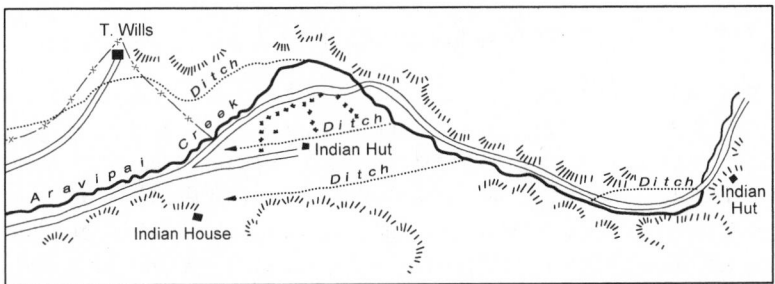

Figure 12. Detail of a 1905 General Land Office map showing Chiquito's farm, noted as "Indian Hut," "Indian House," and "Ditches," situated at Big Sycamore Stands There, the site of the massacre at Camp Grant.

ing. "I have never offered any objection to Chiquito's return, or to his peaceable enjoyment of all the water he could use or needed, for the cultivation of his crops," Waldon wrote. "However scheming neighbors of mine saw their opportunity in this ignorant Indian and actually purchased from Chiquito all right and title to his water, duly attested before a notary, and properly recorded. This bill of sale is made use of not to deprive Chiquito of water, but as a means of defrauding me out of my just rights." Nevertheless, Chiquito apparently said that Waldon had intentionally destroyed ditches and that he "has been mad at me for I want to get my own land. Some time he get shovels and tries to hit me and carry pistol around my house."

Drawn in 1905, the first official General Land Office map of the area where the Camp Grant Massacre occurred shows a network of canals and several "Indian huts" (fig. 12). This was almost certainly the homestead of Chiquito, who by then was known as Bullis, and his relatives, who successfully had this land officially allotted to him on September 26, 1919. One visitor in 1916 described the settlement as having at least twenty-five acres of irrigated fields, fruit trees, lush mesquite stands, and numerous buildings made from log, cane, and brush.[149] In an interview to justify the allotment, Chiquito said that he was born on this land and had lived his entire life there, except for ten years when he was a prisoner of the government. Not many days after the interview, Chiquito died and was buried by the flowing waters of Aravaipa Creek.

This Is Where It Happened

Even families without homes on the San Pedro continued to come, traveling a well-worn trail between the San Carlos agency and Aravaipa Creek. In the spring and summer, gatherers frequently traveled more than forty miles to the southern end of the Galiuro range or Oracle to collect saguaro fruit, acorns, mescal, and other plant materials. The family of Apache elder Della Steele has long traveled as far as Fort Huachuca in Sierra Vista every summer to gather acorns.[150] These collecting areas had been used for generations. As early as 1834, Apache groups were known to have collected saguaro fruit along the western edge of the Santa Catalina Mountains.[151]

Victoria Tapia and her sister Rosalía Salazar Whelan, Mexican American residents in Aravaipa Canyon during the 1900s, befriended the Hooke family, and the sisters fondly recalled spending time together as the Apaches passed by on their gathering expeditions. "Many Apache used to ride down the canyon looking for acorns and saguaro fruit," a historian wrote, following interviews with Victoria Tapia (née Salazar). "One Apache family, the Hooks; father, mother, and a son and daughter, came and would live with the Salazar's for 3 months at a time. . . . Mr. Hook helped with the cattle and Mrs. Hook aided in household chores and weeding the garden."[152] Victoria's older sister, Rosalía Salazar Whelan, also recalled "whole troops" of Apaches arriving on horseback to gather food and Apache children playing games like Ring Around the Rosie.[153] In an interview, Apache elder Howard Hooke recalled a trip he took around 1940 with his grandparents. They traveled from Hawk Canyon southward and camped at an orange grove in the bottom of Aravaipa Canyon. When they reached the San Pedro River several days later, they began gathering saguaro fruit and walnuts. Years later, Howard tried to continue this tradition, but a landowner brandishing a shotgun rebuffed his party of travelers. He never made the journey again.[154]

Although Apaches were not relinquishing their land to the south when they moved to San Carlos in 1873, the intrusion of settlers and prospectors made it difficult for them to protect their interests. With the Apaches' loss of southern territory and their confinement to San Carlos, residents in southern Arizona, particularly those along the

Figure 13. Apache consultants Stevenson Talgo and Howard Hooke discuss the route from San Carlos to Aravaipa Creek, which passes under the cliffs in the distance.

San Pedro River and in Tucson, were able to live in relative peace, having displaced the aboriginal occupants. In this sense, the perpetrators of the Camp Grant Massacre truly achieved what they had hoped: Aravaipa and Pinal Apaches lost many of their loved ones and much of their beloved homeland. And yet, even though Western Apaches have neither the land base in the San Pedro Valley they once had nor easy access to traditional places, they continue to express the deep meanings of this place for them. Some Apache elders remember specific places for both their broad cultural and intensely personal value. Rosalie Talgo, for example, still remembers the graves of her relatives near Big Sunflower Hill.[155] For other elders, recalling place-names in the valley is, as Keith H. Basso wrote, a vital means of place-making, "a way of constructing history itself, of inventing it, of fashioning novel versions of 'what happened here.'"[156] More than sixty Apache place-names have recently been recorded in the San Pedro Valley.[157]

Certainly the past is not unrelated to our future or our present—to the conditions of life on the San Carlos Apache Reservation and the growth of Tucson as a town on the American frontier. These are the traces of the past that connect then to now. But remembering what has happened and how it has shaped our modern landscapes is not always easy. Apache elder Larry Mallow Sr. told Ian Record that his father, Marshall Mallow, an Aravaipa descendant, used to take him to the massacre site. "I came with my father to this place. That's when he would tell the story. He would cry when he told the story," Mallow said. "Sometimes he told the story, sometimes he didn't. It was pretty hard on him. We came to visit just to see the place."[158]

The story of the massacre is a difficult story to tell and to hear. As Francis Cutter explained at a memorial service in 1984, she deeply regretted that she had heard only fragments of the story from her grandmother.[159] She believed that forgetting the past was itself a great loss to her and her people. "My grandmother would say," Cutter recalled, "'Listen to me! Listen to me!' We would be driving the car past here and she would say, 'This is where it happened—a shooting! A killing!' And I wondered what she was talking about. That is the saddest part."

THE HISTORICAL IMAGINATION

"Frequently the motivations were racially induced, but it was almost always through misunderstanding and ignorance and lack of understanding of fellow man," a historian proclaims about massacres along the American frontier at the beginning of "Massacres II," an episode of the television show *Wild West Tech*. Ironically, as this knowing pronouncement is made, a scene unfolds that perpetuates the very kind of misunderstanding and racial stereotyping the historian is condemning. Onscreen, in dramatic slow motion, a snarling Indian in colorful war paint and regalia is brandishing a knife while chasing white women and children as they run for their lives, screaming in terror. The Hollywood Indian attacks again.

Hosted by actor David Carradine, the History Channel program examines four disparate massacres: the Goliad Massacre (1836), which transpired when Mexican soldiers killed more than three hundred Texan rebels; the Council House Massacre (1840), which took the lives of Comanches in San Antonio when a treaty negotiation went awry; the Dragoon Springs Massacre (1858), which involved several workers who killed their bosses at a stagecoach station; and finally the Camp Grant Massacre. Although each event is by definition a massacre—a slaughter and carnage—the perpetrators and victims, as well as the causes and effects, differ dramatically from case to case. By lumping the Camp Grant Massacre with these other events, the program morally and historically equates the 1871 murder of dozens of Apaches with an open war, a spontaneous affray, and an isolated criminal act.

An even more disquieting aspect to this program is its guise of public education. It purports to reveal what *really* happened, when in actuality it only perpetuates the myths of American righteousness and Indian savagery. The story of the massacre at Camp Grant in particular is simplistic and misconstrued. The Apaches are but caricatures. "The Aravaipa Apaches are fierce warriors," Carradine says. "They began knocking off Anglos and Mexicans in a nasty game of survival of the fittest." The overall tone of the program is tactless, as Carradine makes off-color jokes and flirts with "Brittany," a sexy cowgirl who hovers around him between segments. Carradine repeatedly mispronounces key names, such as San Xavier, Eskiminzin, Elías, and Aravaipa. The program's adaptation of the massacre is yet again the Anglo version repeated in accounts from *A Century of Dishonor* to *Oh What a Slaughter*. The massacre is presented for our amusement, not our education.

Remembering and recording the past are fundamental to the human experience.[1] *Wild West Tech* is only the most recent version of storytelling and, in that sense, resembles the documents and oral narratives explored in the previous chapters. Like other communication modes, a television program is an interpretive exercise, a product fashioned from bits of empirical data, memories, conjectures, ideas, and arguments. The interpretive constraints of history result in accounts of past events that are never straightforward and are always in some sense partial and political; as a historical retelling, *Wild West Tech* is not simply entertainment.

The assertion that history is imagined and is not an exact recreation of past events challenges several centuries of Western historiography that have proceeded as if the past is wholly concrete and knowable. Anthropologist Nicholas Thomas has claimed that the "orthodox historical imagination" habitually fails "to acknowledge that versions of the past are always recreated for the here and now, are always politically inflected, partial, and interested."[2] Such arguments have been amply supported by case studies that illustrate the intentional and unintentional manipulations of history for myriad political ends.[3] Conceiving of history as socially constructed does not require us to support an extreme relativist position but to concede that insofar as the "real" past depends on subjective human perceptions, it is not entirely knowable. Even though scholars have begun to recognize that a historical text is necessarily a product of its broader social context, identifying when and how history has been massaged to better fit the zeitgeist of the political present remains a challenge.

When stories such as the Camp Grant Massacre enter a community's collective memory, they become part of the historical imagination, a people's shared vision of the past.[4] Novels or ancient myths may nourish the historical imagination as may scholarly research or family photo albums. When history is written, the text itself becomes a kind of cultural artifact that can help us uncover not only the past as it happened but also the present in which the moments of the past were imagined. Thus historical writings often tell us as much about the world of the author as the world depicted in the text.

While the last two chapters explore the social and historical aspects of the massacre, this chapter investigates how representations of the past, even seemingly innocuous depictions, can be encoded with political meanings. The Camp Grant Massacre is an ideal subject for this analysis because it involves what seems at first to be a single discrete event, written about for over a century by dozens of authors. I endeavor to reveal how historical texts represent more than a range of possible stories; they also expose political machinations and power struggles to elevate a certain version of the past while diminishing competing claims. As seen in the last chapter, I am also deeply concerned with trying to understand the historicity of various accounts, an effort that entails better discerning the biases of the written record. Not only is it important to keep learning from this heartrending event in a general way, it is equally essential to appreciate that the extant corpus of published texts does not provide a transparent window upon an immutable past. Realizing that Western historical texts may not provide the only true history reinforces the importance of multivocality and the need to incorporate the oral histories of native peoples whose own understanding of history has largely been dismissed as unreliable, subjective, and unfixed.[5] If non-native historical texts are similarly afflicted, both ways of knowing the past should arguably be treated with, if not equal skepticism, at least equal consideration.

The Politics of Numbers

Hayden White has argued that historians do not simply reveal the past; they create it through the process of transforming a chronicle of events into intelligible narrative prose.[6] In any given study, the professional historian selects a particular arrangement of events, choosing what to include and exclude, highlight and attenuate. These decisions, White posits, are not self-evident. Even answering the most elementary historical questions of who, what, when, why, and how demands a concentrated effort to compose a cohesive and logical account. The past is not, however, an infinitely plastic resource. Our interpretations of history are constrained by the actual progression of events as well as culturally bound mechanisms that dictate how a society conjures the past.[7]

The historical texts of the Camp Grant Massacre tell many different stories that vary with the author's choice of tone, genre, events, characters, dates, and numbers. After examining archives, libraries, and the Internet, I was able to locate sixty-five texts written between 1871 and 2003.[8] The number of published texts has increased over time, as twenty-one pieces were written in the first half of the period of inquiry, between 1871 and 1937, and at least forty-four were made available in the second half, between 1938 and 2003. The texts constitute a range of print media, including newspaper and journal articles (38), books (5), book sections (9), Web sites (3), and various kinds of manuscripts (10).[9] Though this list is the result of concerted searches at libraries and archives, it undoubtedly does not comprise the entire body of literature on the Camp Grant Massacre but represents at the very least the broad range of available texts. These writings exhibit a shift from news stories to historical analyses and to a miscellany of analyses, news, and fictional accounts. Immediately following the events, the historical texts were largely news items, that is, stories about the event from either eyewitnesses or reporters. Although William Oury presented one version of events to the Society of Arizona Pioneers in 1885, the first in-depth analysis by a professional historian may be George Hammond's 1929 booklet *The Camp Grant Massacre: A Chapter in Apache History*.[10] Hammond's work ushered in a period of more objective historical investigations, combined with a number of newspaper reports rehashing the massacre. The intentional transformation of reality to fancy, nonfiction to fiction, began with Don Schellie's 1968 *Vast Domain of Blood*, an invented narrative based on extensive research. In the last three decades, readers have seen an increasing number of texts in a range of genres, including newspaper articles, magazine commentaries, academic treatments, historical novels, Web sites, and even a romance novel (fig. 14).

Numbers are often considered to be raw facts that exist in the real world as concrete, unassailable objects. Because counts and figures seem to have an absolute nature independent of the writer and reader, numerals are imbued with a distinct sense of authority.[11] In historical texts, numbers are often regarded as a type of bare empirical data, the selected elements of a chronicle that form the foundation for claims of historical truth. While these data may involve biography (she had red hair) or geographical descriptions (he climbed steep cliffs), numerical stipulations (there were twenty-three people) as empirical data may often be seen as more intrinsic to the universe than descriptions such as red hair or steep cliffs, which depend in part on subjective judgments. Red hair could also be described as auburn tresses and steep cliffs could be called vertical crags, whereas 23 people cannot easily be interpreted as 24 people or 22.5 people. Numbers are intuitively conceived of as more concrete than other forms of empirical historical data. As we will see, however, assumptions about the intrinsic truth of certain statistics that may hold in higher mathematics become more problematic when numbers are used to portray social interactions.

With few exceptions, hardly any new empirical data on the Camp Grant Massacre have surfaced in the last century. Indeed, nearly every historical account recycles the first Anglo-American versions of the massacre and proximate events. Writers have notably drawn much material from the very people who were deeply invested in the affair, such as William Oury, John Wasson, and Royal Whitman, who were hardly impartial witnesses. Yet, even as writers have returned repeatedly to the same basic source material, we shall see that the reported numbers associated with the events have shifted in substantial and patterned ways. The varied use of the basic historical data is in part due to the chaos of the events themselves, the uncertainty, even in 1871, of what happened and why. If this were

Figure 14. The cover of *Embrace the Wind*, a romance novel loosely based on the events surrounding the massacre at Camp Grant.

the only source of the discrepancies in empirical data, however, one could expect a random or at least a consistent fluctuation in numbers from 1871 to the present. But instead we see a systematic shift in the empirical data over time. These shifts cannot be explained by an improved understanding of the massacre over time because the number of killed, the number of children captured, and the number of participants remain as uncertain today as they were in 1871. Moreover, these shifts cannot be explained simply by looking at how numbers are represented in different genres—on the assumption that scholars might get numbers right more often than journalists or novelists—for the same basic problem persists: If bare empirical facts exist, should not all writers, whether they be journalists or professors, draw from the same pool of facts to construct their narratives? Historical "facts" are supposed to be incontrovertible, not changeable with the whims of each author.[12]

Reckoning the Dead

Most would say without hesitation that any act of murder, the premeditated killing of an innocent person, is as horrifying as it is deplorable. Our view of murder may vary, however, with the number of victims and the justification for such an act. Thus the way writers have represented the number of people murdered during the Camp Grant Massacre is not incidental. In the historical texts examined here, the number of victims ranges from 30 to 195 and rises between 1871 and 2003.[13] In the immediate aftermath of the massacre, the number killed was uncertain. Given that they initially buried the dead, U.S. Army soldiers stationed at Camp Grant were well positioned to count bodies, but army documents are contradictory, with the number killed escalating from 21 to 30 to 63 to 80 to 100.[14] Some estimates may have been inflated by combining the number of dead with the number of children captured, or they may have equated the number of victims with the 108 legal counts of murder. In the first 66 years after the massacre, from 1871 to 1937, the recorded number of murder victims ranged widely from 30 to 195, while in the subsequent 66 years, the number ranged more narrowly from 75 to 144 Apache victims.

When authors cite a low number of murders and fail to mention the possibility of a higher body count, they are not simply reporting a historical fact—for the "fact" is that the exact total is indeterminate—but are subtly downplaying the violence against the Apaches. Conversely, authors who employ only a high number are suggesting more abominable consequences of the massacre. For instance, in a deposition published in the *Arizona Citizen* a month after the massacre, participant James Lee claimed that he counted thirty-five dead in the aftermath of the attack.[15] The number of victims was not discussed elsewhere in that edition of the *Arizona Citizen*, and accompanying Lee's deposition were articles almost exclusively devoted to justifying the murders. Other editions of the *Arizona Citizen*, however, claimed the number killed was eighty-five, and the *Arizona Miner* reported 125.[16] Significantly, in the month of May, newspapers recorded higher numbers of victims. By June, however, as it became clear that the news of the massacre was not well received in the East, newspapers reported lower numbers until the indictments for murder in October 1871. The apparent vagaries in the number killed, first high and then low, seemed to correlate with the kinds of arguments being made in the months following the massacre.

Even the *same* number can be contextualized differently to convey varied meanings. In a May 27, 1871, article entitled "125 Indians Killed, Righteous Redistribution," the author writes, "we applaud and glorify the deed, and rejoice in the establishment of the reservation in Arivipa Canyon, where 125 good Pinals shall rest without hunger or thirst till resurrection."[17] In contrast, a Web site designed in part to examine the Carrillo legacy cites the same figure of 125 as an admonishment of the Carrillo family for their role in the events surrounding the massacre.[18] In this case, alluding to the higher number is not intended to inspire celebration but censure.

Missing Numbers, Missing Children

One of the many tragedies that followed the morning of April 30, 1871, was the enslavement of Apache children whose parents had either fled the attack or had been murdered. Like the number of those killed, the number of children the attackers abducted has never been clearly established. Hints of the children's fate are scattered in various documents. Evidently some died, some were sold into slavery in Mexico, and some remained in the homes of Tucson families, including the prominent Carrillo and Romero households.[19] Even in 1871 the enslavement of these children was public knowledge; the *Arizona Citizen* and the *Arizona Miner* reported on it three times.[20] The disappearance of the children weighed heavily on the surviving Apaches. Royal Whitman reported that they feared the worst for the children, particularly those sold into slavery.[21] A year later, peace talks almost collapsed when only six children were returned.[22]

According to the historical texts used in this study, somewhere between eleven and thirty-five children were seized following the massacre. Similar to the pattern observed in reports of Apache murder victims, the reported number of abducted children steadily increased over the years, and we see a wider range of numbers before 1937 than after. The fact that some of the children were sold as slaves in Mexico, while others were purchased or "adopted" by some of the most respected families in southern Arizona, as Indian agent Wilbur discovered, were two good reasons for early writers to downplay the captivity. Given the prominence of those complicit in these acts, it is not surprising that only thirty-nine of sixty-five texts (60 percent) mention the number of children abducted, although the number of captives and the identity of certain captors were hardly a secret. The practice of slavery is of course considered contemptible by today's standards, but it had already been outlawed in the United States in 1865, a number of years before the massacre. Thus it is difficult to imagine even a cursory discussion of these events that does not at least mention the captives. The failure of many texts, older and more recent, to confront these facts endorses a silence that assists in the children's erasure from the historical imagination. And when the living no longer recall these lost children, they will have finally and completely disappeared.

Authors who present these numbers not in absolute terms but in ranges or with qualifying provisos reflect the moral and historical ambiguity of the captured children. Most frequently writers offered a single number, but ranges such as "twenty-eight to thirty-two" or qualifiers like "nearly thirty" or "about twenty-eight" also occurred. Looking across different categories of empirical data, we see that the numbers of those killed and captured were least often identified in absolute terms. In 58 percent of the references to the number of Apache killed, a qualifying term or range of numbers was used, and for those captured, ambiguous phrases were used in 25 percent of the descriptions. If we compare these numbers to the number of participants recorded, we observe that qualifying terms were used in 7 percent of the references to Anglo-Americans, in 0 percent to Mexican Americans, and 7 percent to Tohono O'odham participants. The use of absolute numbers seems to more patently render certain aspects of the massacre, yet the true number of participants is just as unclear as the number of murdered and captured. An author's choice to use ranges or qualifying terms is a reasonable approach to acknowledge different versions of the same event and is not in itself problematic, but all of these numbers are in essence equally uncertain. The number of Apache murder victims is no more definitively known than the number of Mexican American participants, and yet writers have presented some numbers as more certain than others. Thus it is significant that the numbers of those murdered and captured are more frequently expressed as uncertainties than other categories of data that are presented as more unequivocal facts.

Scholars of the uses of history have emphasized the importance of considering not only what is added to history but also what is subtracted.[23] An examination of patterns of numerical inclusion and exclusion in descriptions of the massacre reveals a rise in the use of more explicit historical data over the last several decades. Between 1871 and 1937 authors were much less likely to use specific numbers than in later years between 1938 and 2003. Perhaps by excluding the numbers involved in the massacre, particularly the number killed and captured, earlier texts tried to minimize the horrifying violence of the event. We see this tactic early on in a July 1871 newspaper article with the defensive title "The Alleged Arizona Massacre," which avoids any explicit reference to the number of killed. Several later pioneer accounts, such as those of Atanacia Hughes and Charles Wood, similarly leave out such details.[24] A recent example of this tactic is evident in a 1996 online editorial whose author, arguing in defense of the attackers, does not mention the number of Apaches killed and captured.[25] This intentional or unintentional act of historical omission greatly bolsters the author's arguments, for clearly readers who knew the possible number of victims would be less sympathetic to a defense of the attackers. Many of the later texts have, however, highlighted these empirical data, whose implications are significant, and help to explain why we are still talking about the morning of April 30, 1871.

Counting Collusion

The number of participants in the attack is important because the figure indicates the scale of massacre—how many were involved and to what degree. Even some of the participants, however, are not consistent in reporting the number of participants. William Oury's 1879 account stated, "The whole command numbered 140 men, divided as to the nationality as follows; Ninety-two Papago Indians, 42 Mexicans, and six Americans."[26] The number grew slightly in 1885 when Oury presented a paper before the Society of Arizona Pioneers: "Papagoes 92, Mexicans 48, Americans 6, in all 146 men good and true."[27] Oury's tally of Mexican participants is not the only number to experience an increase. Figures have risen over the years in each main category of empirical data, with the exception of Tohono O'odham participants, whose numbers have decreased slightly.

Despite such ambiguities of data, many authors cite these and other numbers as "facts," offering claims of anywhere between 100 and 154 attackers. Many authors describe at length the ethnic mix of the attackers and the dynamic among them. Several texts repeat Oury's assertion that when the different groups first met, Jesús María Elías, a rival leader, ridiculed Oury by declaring that his "countrymen are grand on resoluting and speechifying, but when it comes to action they show up exceedingly thin."[28] What was an embarrassment for Oury is a recurring theme in texts that often contrast the number of Anglo-American participants with the number of Mexican Americans and even more frequently with the number of Tohono O'odham. Writers consistently put the number of Anglo-Americans at six while the number of Mexican American and O'odham conspirators varies, even though all these data are equally unsubstantiated. Of the forty-four texts that cite the number of Anglo-American participants, forty-two (95 percent) quote the number as six. (The other two texts posit five and seven Anglo-Americans.) Similarly, authors place the number of Mexican American collaborators at forty-eight 86 percent of the time. References to the O'odham are more inconsistent, ranging from 92 to 100 participants. Of the texts that cite a specific figure, 51 percent give the number of Tohono O'odham as 92, 27 percent claim 94 O'odham participants, 12 percent cite 100, and smaller percentages use 93, 95, and 98. While such variability in the O'odham and Mexican American head count is not in itself that large, it stands out in stark contrast to the consistency with which the number of Anglo-Americans is set at six.

Undoubtedly, six Anglo-Americans would have been easier for witnesses to count, recall, and document than scores of Mexican Americans and O'odham combatants. Furthermore, the first written sources were authored predominantly by Anglo-Americans, who arguably would have been more likely to recognize and care about the Anglo-American participants than the more culturally distant O'odham and Mexican Americans. Although there is a distinct possibility that the number of Anglo-American participants is uniformly six because it was the actual number, this figure does not stand uncontested. Atanacia Santa Cruz Hughes, whose husband, Samuel Hughes, supplied rifles and other provisions for the attack, stated in 1926, "Juan Elias was one of the leaders and of course Bill Oury was the leader of them all. . . . I don't know how many Americans went. I am sure there were more than six."[29] On the witness stand at the murder trial, participant Charles Tanner Etchels, a blacksmith, suggested that all those indicted were in the attacking party: "So far as I know the names of them, I think all of the defendants were with the party from Tucson to the San Pedro."[30] On the other hand, participant James Lee, a mill operator and silver mine owner, stated in sworn testimony that the accused did not fully represent the actual participants: "There are parties indicated who were not there at all. [Only] a portion of them were those indicted."[31]

Calculated across various historical texts, the average number of *total* participants irrespective of ethnicity is 142. Yet these same texts steadily report that only 100 individuals were put on trial, leaving a gap of some forty people to be accounted for and explained. Although I do not necessarily subscribe to a conspiracy theory, there are nevertheless some tantalizing clues that suggest intentional obfuscation by accomplices in the massacre.[32] For instance, Leander Spofford allegedly declared in an interview, "All participating in that raid swore to never state who took part in it. . . . I will tell the story and mention no names other than those who have told of their part in it."[33] And a historian reported an exchange years after the massacre with William Bailey, who claimed, "There were a great many more men in that party—W. S. Oury and Jesus Maria Elias originated it. I signed an oath and promised never to tell anything about it or tell the name of anybody that took part in it; but as twenty years have passed since then, I think I am at liberty to speak about it."[34] Thus documentary evidence casts some suspicion on a total of only six Anglo-American participants. Significantly, this uncertainty fails to be acknowledged in the historical texts of the Camp Grant Massacre.

Six is also an unsettling total in that it draws attention only to those Tucsonans who we know took up arms against innocent Apaches that April morning: William Oury, Sidney DeLong, Charles Etchells, James Lee, D. A. Bennett, and John Foley.[35] But many others were architects of this violence—planting the seeds of hatred, enabling the murders to unfold, and justifying the unjustifiable in its aftermath. Sidney DeLong, Jésus María Elías, William Oury, Samuel Hughes, A.P.K. Safford, Hiram Stevens, and John Wasson were all guilty conspirators, and even though some may have never fired a shot, as Tucson's leading businessmen they all stood to gain from the prolongation of the Apache conflict.[36] In addition, numerous Tucsonans celebrated the homecoming of the murderers; a dozen Tucsonans on the jury betrayed their duty to assure that justice was done; and much of Tucson rewarded DeLong, "an honorable and upright man," by electing him their mayor in 1872.[37] Although these Tucsonans may be less blameworthy than Elías or Oury, they are not without guilt. The number six so simply and cleanly denies any greater culpability.

Variability in the data may be due in part to the ways in which race and ethnicity are represented in the texts. The O'odham, in particular, play an ambiguous role in the event. They are frequently portrayed through the twin stereotypes of Noble Indian and Savage Indian, a contradictory dual image propagated since the earliest days of colonial contact.[38] Jerry O'Neil succinctly captures this duality in his description of nineteenth-century attitudes toward the Tohono

O'odham: "The Papagos were known to be peaceful Indians, but they were still Indians," meaning that even nonviolent Indians have some kind of core ferocity innate to *all* Indians.[39] In Elliott Arnold's historical novel *The Camp Grant Massacre*, he describes the Tohono O'odham waiting in quiet repose when the attackers first assembled: "The Papago young men, who could not as yet be called Enemy Killers, were gathered along the bank of the Rillito when Bill Oury rode up. They were dressed in white cotton. They were sitting on the ground, their legs crossed under them, their faces turned toward the morning sun, their heads bowed. . . . No one talked. No one looked up when Bill Oury's horse brought him up to the pleasant river-bank."[40] The Tohono O'odham thus exude a kind of stoic serenity in Arnold's original portrait. But underneath the O'odham façade of tranquil nobility beats the heart of a savage killer, which Arnold portrays in his subsequent descripton of the attack on the Apache rancheria: "Don Guillermo [William Oury] had cautioned them [the Papagos] to use their clubs first, to kill as many of the Enemy as possible before the village was aroused. The Papagos took that as a needless command. Bullets were impersonal. What joy was there in slaying an enemy from a long way away?"[41]

Arnold depicts the acts of the Tohono O'odham as systematically and ruthlessly violent. Based on the recollections of Oury and other participants, historical texts almost always place the Tohono O'odham at the forefront of the intense carnage and horrific slaughter, while the Anglo-Americans and Mexican Americans sit on a nearby ridge coolly shooting at fleeing Apaches. "That many of the [Apache] women and children were killed by the Papagos is probable," as one historian wrote, "this was one of the drawbacks of having Indian allies."[42] Moreover, placing the O'odham at the front of the assault implies their greater responsibility for the rapes and mutilations. Elliott Arnold, as well as Don Schellie and others, understood this inference and openly attributed the rapes that Dr. Briesly reported to the O'odham, which only further reinforced Arnold's depictions of the O'odham's savage traits.[43] Yet to my knowledge Briesly never suggested who among the assailants committed these acts.[44]

The descriptions of the attack in historical texts have been almost entirely from the perspective of Anglo-Americans who had a vested interest in placing the murders squarely on the Tohono O'odham. But historical documents suggest more extensive Anglo and Mexican American involvement. For instance, as noted in chapter 3, an Anglo-American man later reported that during the attack he personally used a saber to kill Apaches.[45] And Sherman Curley, readers will recall from chapter 2, told Grenville Goodwin, "I ran into an arroyo. I had my bow and arrows, and I pointed at them as if I was going to shoot. This scared some Mexicans and Papagoes back, who were after me."[46]

When the historical texts do not challenge previously published accounts and place the O'odham on the front lines of the battle, they highlight the responsibility of the O'odham and obscure the involvement of Anglo-Americans and Mexican Americans. In part, the number of Anglo-American participants has remained so constant in historical texts because the authors can intimate that Anglo-Americans undoubtedly played a part in the massacre, but *only* six people participated—no fewer perhaps, but certainly no more. This number is implicitly contrasted with the Mexican Americans and especially the Tohono O'odham, who not only purportedly far outnumbered the Anglo-Americans but also committed most of the atrocities. Yet, at the same time, the O'odham are described as a peaceful people who murder only out of necessity. Perhaps one reason the Tohono O'odham numbers vary is the ambiguous dual role they have been assigned as both Savage and Noble Indian.

History as a Contested Field

Geographer David Lowenthal once suggested that history, as the story of what has gone before, is simultaneously "less than the past" and "more than the past."[47] History is less than the past because it turns on the biases of the storyteller and the listener, who cannot objectively replicate past events in their infinite entirety and complexity. At the same time, history is more than the past because "it is organized by and filtered through individual minds. . . . subjective interpretation gives it life and meaning."[48] Thus, historians and their audiences together weave the strands of a real past into a story that has value and vitality.

In this chapter I have tried to show that history is not just an empty stage on which any tale may be performed. Rather, historical texts constitute a domain of competing claims, each vying for legitimacy at distinct social and historical moments. This assertion resonates with Nicholas Thomas, who wrote, "The cultural differences between different narratives emerge from political situations, from interests in particular constructions of the past. What confronts us is not merely a plurality of accounts, but a contested field."[49] Indeed, as we come to appreciate the fluidity of the Camp Grant Massacre data, we see that even numbers do not present inviolable truths but exist as mutable and contested constructions, which are nonetheless essential to stories of the past imagined in the political present.

5

HISTORY, MEMORY, JUSTICE

At the end of April 1984, some seventy-five people gathered not far from the ruins of Camp Grant to remember and commemorate the massacre and its victims. Messages were read from Massachusetts senator Edward Kennedy and Arizona representative Morris K. Udall, as well as a letter from governor Bruce Babbitt, who declared April 30, 1984, Apache Memorial Day. At one point in the ceremony, two air force jets streamed by only five hundred feet above the ground, tilting their wings in unison as they passed.

Several Apache leaders and community members stepped forward to share their feelings, a mix of sadness about the past and hope for the future. A young woman named Winema Dewey, a descendant of *haské bahnzin*, expressed the grief surely felt by many, but she also suggested that, by joining together, people could make some sense of this tragic past. "We should come together," she said, "and try to make an effort . . . that we understand what happened here. . . . We shouldn't try to bury it. . . . it's like turning over a rock."[1] Other speeches revealed the complexities involved in recalling and commemorating such a terrible event. "Although the Camp Grant Massacre will live forever in the memory of the Apache people," Apache elder Philip Cassadore said, we are gathered here neither to forgive nor to condemn." Then he added: "The past is gone."[2] By this I think Cassadore meant that Apaches may never recover what was lost so many years ago, that perhaps we should not dwell on past injustices. Ronnie Lupe, then White Mountain Apache tribal chairman, emphasized the continuity of the past and present. "It is not forgotten, it is here with us," he said.[3]

Several stories concerning how Apaches learned of the massacre suggest the lingering personal and social anxiety that surrounds the event. Young Howard Hooke had passed the site of the massacre on an annual trip through Aravaipa Creek with his grandparents, who did not speak of the event for fear it would bring them bad luck on the journey.[4] Similarly, Norbert Pechulie used to travel each summer up Aravaipa Creek with his father, Sampson, and they would stop by *gashdla'á cho o'aa*. "He showed me where the massacre was, but he didn't really talk too much about it," Pechulie recalled. "He never really said anything about it."[5] Winema Dewey said that she did not learn of the massacre until she was 22 years old. Francis Cutter, as noted in chapter 3, only heard bits and pieces of the story from her grandmother, who spoke of it only in a general way: "This is where it happened—a shooting, a killing!" her elderly grandmother exclaimed when they passed the massacre site. Jeanette Cassa once explained in an interview that many Apaches are in some sense reluctant to resurrect the past. "That was the past and you didn't look back," she said. "You're a gravedigger then—digging up the past. You buried them and it's like digging them back up. We were taught like that, so we're apprehensive to talk about these things. It was bad to do that. We didn't even mention the dead's name."[6]

And yet, these same people often show a strong desire to remember the massacre, reflect upon its meanings, and hear the story told from Apache perspectives.[7] This longing is in evidence in the few memorial services Apaches organized in the 1980s and 1990s. In 1995 some Apaches started a campaign to have a memorial erected near Highway 77, "not to open old wounds . . . but simply to include the Apache version of what happened," according to Apache historian Dale C. Miles.[8] "We just want people to know their relatives were massacred and there's nothing in the history books about what happened here," said San Carlos resident Salton Reede Jr. at the 1982 memorial ceremony, commenting on the lack of Apache viewpoints.[9] At the same ceremony, Philip Cassadore said that Apaches have been treated unfairly in the past and must in the future "speak for themselves."[10] The oral histories and traditions related in chapter 2 attest to the presence of multiple and dynamic Apache points of view on the massacre even though these perspectives have been ignored in the official history recycled by scholars, journalists, and novelists through the years. Among Apaches these stories have never been fully forgotten, repressed, or erased by collective amnesia despite a certain ambivalence they express toward the past. This tension was perhaps captured symbolically at the 1984 memorial ceremony in which two women danced, taking four steps forward, then three steps back.[11]

Anthropologist Michael Jackson, who did extensive fieldwork in Sierra Leone before and after its recent civil war, provides one way to think about these conflicting attitudes, positing that the "past" is essentially a cultural strategy that people use to filter their present experiences. In this view we cannot assume that traumatic events of long ago "leave permanent psychic scars whose repercussions continue to be felt, like original sin, unto the seventh generation."[12] Jackson argues that when we see the present flowing from the past inevitably and naturally, when we see only causative forces beyond human control, individual historical actors escape our moral judgments. We are left simply with victims and perpetrators who do not make their world but rather are made by it.

Jackson asserts that historical memories and shared stories of violence preserve "traces of two quite different strategies of coping with violence—vengeance and forgiveness—and so leave open, at all times, the possibility of choosing how one will react to evil."[13] The ways people choose to think and talk about the past have both positive and negative features that are manifest in modes of grievance and acceptance. The grievance mode is positive, according to Jackson, when it aids the bereavement process and serves as a way to deal with loss and separation. In more extreme and negative forms, however, these behaviors "become habitual ways of addressing the world, and as such, feed fantasies of revenge, encourage the idealization of the lost object, and, by holding a person in thrall to the past, prevent creative reengagement with the world."[14] Jackson offers the example of an actual army corporal named Sankoh, who "is so in thrall to his *ressentiment* that nothing can cure him of it. More imperative even than power was this self-defeating need to keep his hatred alive."[15] Acceptance, the other mode, may help people understand the practical limits of their actions, but in excess the acceptance mode may cause debilitating depression and apathy or, as Pierre Bourdieu wrote, a "fatalistic submission to the forces of the world."[16]

Jackson's research offers insight into the ways that people elect to think and talk about the past can affect their lives in the present. The Apache viewpoints expressed at the memorial ceremonies are situated somewhere between the poles of staggering grief and bleak acquiescence, blending modes of grievance and acceptance. In the collective memory of past violence, Jackson writes, are the seeds of both revenge and atonement. But the ambiguity of history's meaning emerges as individuals toil to plant future hopes in a soil untainted by the frustration of unrealized revenge or the despair of offering absolution to the unrepentant. "We are gathered here neither to forgive nor to condemn," Philip Cassadore said. While it is important to understand that history is an interpretive act realized in the present, we also need to recognize that our reconstructions of past violence are not *merely* modes of performance. The present really is produced by the past—today is in many ways what it is because of yesterday—even as the past is re-produced in the present through stories and history books.

If historical scholarship is just another way of dealing with the past, then what may be said of Apache narratives is equally true of scholarly accounts. Some thorny questions thus arise from this book: In which mode do anthropological histories of massacres operate? Is this book in the grievance or acceptance mode, or somewhere in between? Will this research on the Camp Grant Massacre only re-open the proverbial old wounds? Or, since this event happened so long ago, does it merely offer a forlorn acceptance of what cannot be changed? And these initial questions lead to yet more fundamental ones: What can be gained from studying massacres and genocides? Is this kind of research historical voyeurism or, worse, as Cassa said, "gravedigging"? If not undertakers and grave robbers, what are ethnohistorians? Should we not focus on advancing society rather than miring it in the past? *Can* we move forward without the past? Why try to understand the past at all?

When Past Is Present

"The present is what exists and all that is not present does not exist. The past does not exist," wrote Jean Paul Sartre, expressing a radical view of the past as immaterial.[17] Such skepticism about the past's existence and utility can be countered with arguments that acknowledge the past's enduring relevance and service, a view perhaps best expressed by George Santayana's famous maxim "Those who fail to remember the past are doomed to repeat it." Yet Sartre's vision is incomplete because it fails to consider how the past suffuses the present, and Santayana's pronouncement is misleading because every event is a unique happening that can never wholly repeat itself, a fingerprint in time.

I maintain that understanding the past is of fundamental value to individuals and communities for at least three related reasons. First, the contemporary world is not independent of the past. This argument is perhaps most compelling at the individual level, for our identities, our very sense of being, are formed from the past—like a river that is both shaped by and shapes the sand beneath it. "One does not pass through time, but time enters upon him, in his place," wrote the poet N. Scott Momaday. "Notions of the past and future are essentially notions of the present. In the same way an idea of one's ancestry and posterity is really an idea of the self."[18] What is lost when children who attend Sam Hughes Elementary are unaware that their school's namesake supplied the guns used to kill Apaches? Why should it matter if hikers on Wasson Peak know that John Wasson's invectives provoked and vindicated the slaughter of Apaches who had committed no crime? Momaday might respond that if we define our selves through our past, then memories built on falsehoods and fantasies mean a person does not, and cannot, know her or his own self. The importance of the past deepens when we consider not only individuals but also structures of power and social organizations that endure beyond any one lifetime and, indeed, establish relationships among generations. The collective force of institutions and practices such as slavery, industrialization, or democracy exceeds any one individual and inherently involves the dimension of time. Thus to understand our world, both at the individual and collective level, we need to understand something about the past.

The second reason involves the ways in which knowledge of the past can lead to social action in the present. Steven L. Point, a Stó:lo leader from the Northwest Coast, makes this observation about outsiders' reactions to learning about his tribe's difficult past: "When people hear the history, when people understand what has happened, they ask, 'What can we do? How can we make things right? What's reasonable given the situation?'"[19] The power of history and historical stories resides in their capacity to provoke positive change. Howard Zinn has cautioned, however, that "history is not inevitably useful."[20] In other words, knowledge of the past does not necessarily lead to positive social action. Consider, for example, how only a year after the Holocaust Memorial Museum opened in Washington, D.C., a place built to embody the maxim "never again," Americans sat idly by as the genocide in Rwanda unfolded.[21] Nevertheless, Zinn has persuasively argued that at its radical best, history encourages empathy, inspiring us to make a positive difference even as we become aware of our limitations:

> History can untie our minds, our bodies, our disposition to move—to engage life rather than contemplating it as an outsider. It can do this by widening our view to include the silent voices of the past, so that we look behind the silence of the present. It can illustrate the foolishness of depending on others to solve the problems of the world—whether the state, the church, or other self-proclaimed benefactors. It can reveal how ideas are stuffed into us by the powers of our time, and so lead us to stretch our minds beyond what is given. It can inspire us by recalling those few moments in the past when men did behave like human beings, to prove that it is *possible*. And it can sharpen our critical faculties so that even while we act, we think about the dangers created by our own desperation.[22]

These two arguments about the nature of history are grounded on the notion that the past is not simply linked to the present but attains force when it is *made* present. That is to say, history is most valuable not when it is examined for its pastness but when its *relationship* to our lives today is made apparent. The third reason for trying to understand history, the concern we share for justice, arises from this same spirit.

History and Justice

The study of past violence is closely allied to notions of justice. Although social scientists have been increasingly concerned with violence as a cultural practice and have studied how violence is remembered, misremembered, and forgotten, surprisingly few explicitly discuss how re-tracing past events is a means of engaging in justice. To consider this value of history, we must consider the cultural contexts in which "justice" is enacted and some broader questions of political philosophy—that is, not only how justice is pursued but also how it *ought* to be pursued. I begin this inquiry by focusing on the role of history in three different forms of justice: distributive, retributive, and restorative.

Distributive justice for political philosophers most often involves questions about how to resolve present inequalities, such as the unequal distribution of wealth, heath care, or education in a society. Most philosophers who have addressed the role of history in distributive justice have argued that wrongs committed long ago should not factor into our modern moral equations. Jeremy Waldron, for example, contends that historical injustices cannot be fully compensated in the present.[23] When we try to offer reparations to descendants of people who were wronged long ago, we engage in "counterfactual reasoning," which involves speculating on what might have happened had certain events not occurred. To determine, for example, an equitable distribution of goods today, we must somehow calculate the losses people have suffered because of particular wrongs. This line of thinking, Waldron argues, is fraught with difficulties because discovering what *might* have been at any given recent moment, never mind over generations, is unfeasible. Waldron also discusses how modern circumstances may *supersede* past injustices. Imagine, for example, that a family's well was dishonestly appropriated by a government. It seems right to try to return the family's well so long as there are many wells to be had and enough water for all. But in the event of a catastrophic drought, it would seem right that, rather than allowing many to die of thirst, everyone should be able to draw from the well the family formerly held even though it had been unfairly taken from them. Entitlements to various resources change with changing circumstances and contexts of use. Although Waldron recognizes that symbolic gestures of reparation are important and that history may spur us to pursue justice in the present, "it is the impulse to justice now that should lead the way in this process," he says, "not the reparation of something whose wrongness is understood primarily in relation to conditions that no longer obtain."[24]

The philosopher David Lyons makes very similar arguments in his examination of the theft of Native American lands, suggesting that reparation is best argued on the grounds of past injustices that continue to the present day rather than claims of original occupancy.[25] George Sher also believes that the issue of current inequalities is a more compelling argument than ancient claims and posits a "progressive diminution" of claims following an injustice. That is, compensation should be made to those who were directly wronged, but each successive generation has less right to compensation.[26]

These philosophical arguments are not without material consequence. Sociologist Rhoda E. Howard-Hassman compared reparation claims made by Japanese Americans and African Americans and found that the moral factors highlighted by political philosophers may be relevant to outcomes.[27] She discovered that the claims for reparation that Japanese Americans made because of their internment during World War II were largely successful because most victims were still alive, the perpetrators were not diffuse, and the causal chain of harm was relatively short and straightforward. Moreover, the reparations made—an official admission of misbehavior in 1988 and $20,000 to each living victim—did not put unreasonable burdens on the American government or its citizenry. The claims of reparation many African American groups are making for slavery fail to meet these conditions: the most immediate victims are deceased, the perpetrators are diffuse, and slavery's causal chain of harm is long and complex.[28] As many of these claims are relatively new, however, the role of history in distributive justice is yet unresolved from both a philosophical and sociological perspective. Future work by scholars and future efforts by activists will undoubtedly help clarify how we think about history and compensatory justice.

Retributive justice typically involves direct punishment of those who have behaved wrongly. Expressed metaphorically in the aphorism "an eye for an eye," retributive measures are most effectively determined in criminal courts. This kind of justice cannot legitimately be sought with respect to ancient wrongs, however, because the original perpetrators are beyond the punitive reach of later generations.

Although certain descendants may have benefited from the original crimes, to punish them if they are innocent in every other way cannot satisfy our sense of retributive justice; those most guilty have escaped by the fact of their deaths. Furthermore, criminal trials alone often cannot provide justice after mass violence because trials tend to focus on individuals and single acts instead of the broader role of institutional and state forces.[29] The limits of tribunals can be seen in the quick trial and hanging of Adolf Eichmann, for example, a man who enabled the Final Solution to wipe out millions during the Holocaust. On such a scale, the eye-for-an-eye logic seems hollow.[30] As Harold Kaplan observed about the trials following World War II, "The accused at Nuremberg were more than slightly comic. The very size of their crimes reduced them and added a pain to memory that we hardly expected."[31] Criminal trials—which must follow strict rules of evidence and argument—are limited and highly dependent on the political context in which they take place. The trial in the winter of 1871 that prosecuted DeLong and his 99 codefendants for murder was a travesty of justice, not its realization.

In short, retributive justice, like restorative justice to be discussed below, is a kind of reparative justice in that it seeks repair for some socio-psychological, physical, or economic damage done in the past. But in cases of mass violence that occurred in distant ages, retributive justice is inadequate, for a number of reasons: Those most guilty and most wronged are deceased; the scale of such transgressions implicates hosts of people; material compensation may simply never be an adequate reimbursement for some crimes; and retribution often depends on legal frameworks for its realization.

The Healing of Breaches, the Redressing of Imbalances

Restorative justice, which engages history in unique ways, emerged most prominently in the wake of South African apartheid. After decades of gruesome violence, the post-apartheid government concluded that wounds would best be healed by an open and transparent accounting of the past. This was no simple task. Desmond Tutu, a prominent figure in this process, observed that since apartheid ended through treaty and compromise, no party could claim a "victor's justice." Holding Nuremberg-like trials, which followed from the unconditional surrender of the Axis powers to end World War II, would be untenable. Also problematic was the institution-alized character of the violence of apartheid, which required pun-ishment to focus on more than simply a few individuals. Moreover, even if the victims could readily forgive and forget, a national am-nesia, Tutu reasoned, would "in effect be to victimize the victims of Apartheid a second time around. We would have denied some-thing that contributed to the identity of who they were." The result-ing Truth and Reconciliation Commission (TRC) instead sought a "third way" to "rehabilitate and affirm the dignity and personhood of those who for so long had been silenced, and had been turned into anonymous, marginalized ones."[32]

Anthropologists Nancy Scheper-Hughes and Philippe Bourgois offer a partially correct description of the TRC as "a complicated po-litical gamble in which justice is traded for truth," but they also fail to recognize how truth revealed is itself a powerful form of justice.[33] As several observers have noted, "Properly understood, a just and moral appraisal of the past is the true life-blood of reconciliation." Tutu suggests that justice is withheld if conceived of as principally retributive. The TRC instead sought a restorative justice deeply con-cerned with "the healing of breaches, the redressing of imbalances, the restoration of broken relationships, a seeking to rehabilitate both the victim and the perpetrator."[34]

The TRC was to some extent built on the belief that giving vic-tims a voice and the opportunity to narrate their own stories in pub-lic would enable society as a whole to move beyond its sorrowful past. The research of legal scholar Teresa Godwin Phelps supports this theory, revealing how social and corporeal violence imperil not only people's dignity and autonomy but also their ability to articu-late their sufferings. Phelps concludes that any balancing of justice must also be a restoration of language. Giving a voice to the voice-less surpasses mere storytelling; it is fundamental to the ongoing process of justice and reconciliation. "Justice requires a balancing (an accounting), that something taken from the victim of the injus-tice must be restored, be given back," Phelps argues. "The balancing that truth reports afford victims begins to put the world back in order. The victims retrieve the ability to speak and shape their own stories."[35]

Primo Levi reminds us that the perpetrators of mass violence often intentionally bury the truth of history. Hence, when the truth about past violence remains hidden and obscured, the perpetrators remain in a very real sense triumphant.[36] This is certainly true of the Camp Grant Massacre, as discussed in chapter 4, in which the past has been constructed to relate politically biased versions of the event. Reconciliation does not demand one truth to which everyone must subscribe, nor does it entail a relegation of the painful past to the far recesses of collective memory. Instead, the multivocality that emerges from truth commissions should be viewed as a process of engagement that entwines the past with the present through enduring memories.[37] History in this form is a dialogue that critically approaches varying versions of the past while nevertheless aspiring to uncover the truth of events and experiences.

Its grand goals of restorative justice notwithstanding, the South African TRC has been criticized for focusing too heavily on reconciliation at the expense of truth and justice.[38] The TRC's final report explicitly recognized four types of truth, only one of which involved the idea of true statements that correspond to reality. Other critiques allege that quasi-legal proceedings offered uneven amnesty, and while the impressive 21,000 recorded statements provided redemption for some, this number did not even begin to approach the millions of people who suffered under apartheid.[39] An appraisal by Mahmood Mamdani asserts that the TRC focused on traumas of individuals, whereas apartheid as a "crime against humanity" fundamentally involved *institutionalized* discrimination that resulted in the racial and ethnic cleansing of minority groups.[40] Other scholars have similarly argued that truth commissions are often troubled by the mandate to explain "macro-truths" of violence, such as oppressive legal and political structures, through the "micro-truths" of individual experiences of oppression.[41]

Informal Restorative Justice

The most expansive effort to address the wrongs committed against Native Americans in the United States has been the Indian Claims Commission, which arose from the multitude of legal claims the government was facing for land theft and treaty violations. There is, however, no TRC on the horizon to investigate the violent and systemic transgressions against indigenous peoples in North America. TRCs are geared ideally toward transitional societies, nations emerging from situations of extreme conflict into more democratic conditions.[42] Still, the goals of restorative justice may be achieved through other methods. The TRC is one formal system of restorative justice, but I suggest that the *informal* means offered by public memorials, museum exhibits, and history books can also become vehicles for restorative justice. Informal methods, efforts that lack governmental authority and coercive powers, have their own possibilities and pitfalls, but they relate powerfully to the question posed earlier: Why study terrible past events such as the Camp Grant Massacre?

Histories that seek informal restorative justice aspire to some kind of social balance through the realization of the truth. Truth is by no means a simple concept. Recognizing the very complexity of past events, their many causes and consequences, becomes essential in this mode. Too often regimes of power reduce the truth to tidy boundaries between Good and Evil and to polarized categories of Us versus Them. But restorative justice, whatever its method, needs a strong commitment to the ideal of truth—that the past, however messy and complex, really happened and really can be understood. A restorative justice that obscures the truth fails in its express goal of shining a light on the shadows of history and revealing that which has remained perversely hidden.[43]

The restoration of truth is in most ways a symbolic act, since truth is neither an object that can be offered as material reparation nor a weapon that can be wielded to inflict pain. Nevertheless, this symbolic act is not without import and influence. Symbols of the past resonate powerfully in the present. Consider, for example, the Genbaku Dome, now a part of the Hiroshima Peace Memorial, a rich symbol of the devastation of war. Exposing concealed truths can also have significant consequences, such as the public restoration of dignity to victims or, conversely, the public incitement of shame for the guilty. In the same way that courts must establish certain facts before deciding punishment or compensation, determining truth can also precede and lead to material compensation, as Howard-Hassman has shown in the case of Japanese American reparations.[44]

Of the several prominent features that characterize research within the framework of restorative justice, one of the most important is its recognition and elaboration of the phantom histories described in chapter 1, those haunting past events that we understand in a vague rather than a substantial way. "The forgetting of violence is inextricably linked to the remembrance of violence because traumatic experiences are characterized by the inability to be either completely recalled or completely forgotten," as Antonius C.G.M. Robben has observed. "It is precisely this obstruction to either total recall or total erasure, and the unending search for comprehensive understanding, that makes trauma so indigestible and memory so obsessive."[45] Restorative justice hopes to mend collective memory through dialogue that makes sense of the past and balances recall with erasure.

History in the mode of restorative justice is deeply concerned with healing breaches and subsequently is less interested in assigning blame or delineating good and bad in absolute terms. This approach to history recognizes the moral ambiguities of violence, what Primo Levi called the "gray zone," an area that is "poorly defined, where the two camps of masters and servants both diverge and converge." In the gray zone, victims of violence may become prosecutors of violence and vice versa, Levi argues, even as he urges us not to confuse the innocent and the guilty. Regarding the Holocaust, he asserts that the "murderers existed, not only in Germany, and still exist, retired or on active duty, and that to confuse them with their victims is a moral disease or an aesthetic affection or a sinister sign of complicity." Nevertheless, Levi has witnessed and acknowledges how "compassion and brutality can coexist in the same individual in the same moment, despite all logic."[46]

While perhaps a limited concept, the gray zone at least recognizes the contradictions inherent in the difficult decisions people make in periods of extreme conflict and violence. This perspective helps us understand the social and psychological complexity of someone like Lieutenant Whitman, who aggressively defended the Apaches at Camp Grant while also declaring "the vigorous measures to be taken for their extermination" if they did not capitulate. Or consider Leopoldo Carrillo and Francisco Romero, who thought it morally acceptable to abduct children from their families but considered it "an outrage upon Christianity and civilization to force them back into the savage heathenism of the Apaches." Or think of *haské bahn-zin*, who certainly raided blameless settlers yet also suffered horribly under the oppression of American colonialism. Following this logic, one might ask whether a man like Oury should be blamed for his actions. Levi, I believe, would consider the degree to which Oury was coerced and the repercussions of his choices. Oury's actions in the massacre were not coerced, I maintain, and his choices resulted in appalling consequences for many innocent people. Oury was not a cog in the machine, but the machine's master—its designer, maker, and engine. While it remains possible to make this kind of moral assessment, the concept of the gray zone suggests that we also consider the context in which people find themselves and must live.[47]

The work of anthropologists and historians can play a particularly important role in addressing one of the shortcomings of formal TRCs, that is, linking macro- and micro-levels of events, experiences, processes, and structures. Ethnohistorical methods can expose hidden truths and reveal at the same time how history is itself constructed and often employed as a cultural strategy in political settings. Paul Farmer has argued that understanding the relationship between individuals and the structural violence that surrounds them is essential. He posits that one of the best ways to demystify organized violence is an examination of individual stories through which we "learn to see the connections between personal experience, psychological experience, cognition, and affect on the one hand, and the political economy of brutality on the other. It is the political economy of brutality that impelled these horrible events and then played themselves out forever in the lives of people."[48]

In this approach, scholars are not saviors or heroes but participants whose disciplinary training allows them to offer insights while encouraging the larger community to engage in positive dialogue. Every culture deals with the painful past in particular ways, and restorative justice should not supplant local remedies. Because violence on the scale of massacres and genocides is so often *inter-cultural*, however, restorative justice approaches reconciliation through dialogue that fosters cross-cultural conversation and understanding. The Camp Grant Massacre bears most directly on Apache history, but all the people of southern Arizona are implicated if for no other reason than the fact that the event helped secure American hegemony in the region, which allowed for the development of what are now modern Tucson, Sierra Vista, Benson, Mammoth, Dudleyville, and Oracle.

One possible limitation of restorative justice, centered as it is on the symbolic, is that victims or their descendants may not feel that justice has been achieved unless material compensation has been provided. Some will inevitably insist that the only effective antidotes for the loss of land, homes, or lives are economic. Some may say that justice is not fundamentally about reconciliation but about ensuring that someone "pay" for the crimes committed. This line of thinking can encourage us, however, to wallow in the grievance mode by demanding the return of that which is irretrievable. No moral elixir can resurrect the dead, victims or perpetrators. Some misappropriated lands have been so transformed that they are no longer the same places. And what price can we ultimately put on our home, our family, our way of life? Money can simply never compensate for some losses. This does not mean, however, that victims or their descendants should always compromise. In fact, restorative justice can feasibly augment compensatory justice or, in cases of recent violence, retributive justice. But to avoid losing ourselves in an abyss of acrimony, our ideals of justice should be tempered by the practical realities of our circumstances.

The truth is not easy to uncover, and once revealed it does not necessarily lead to reconciliation.[49] Tim Kelsall realized this in Sierra Leone after watching the country's truth commission in session for a week. He found that most of the witnesses "circled around the truth," denied everything, or patently lied. Only after the formal proceedings, in a public ceremony of repentance and forgiveness— a local device for making amends—were the participants able to achieve some measure of reconciliation.[50] Although the truth does not readily reveal itself, truth commissions at least grapple openly with veracity rather than surrendering to the fictions that buttress violence. The truth alone does not necessarily compel people to act, and surely, in some cases of reconciliation, the unearthing of certain truths may be less beneficial than other methods of atonement, such as ritual. But as seen in Sierra Leone, both the public ceremony and the commission aspired to the same end, a justice deeply committed to mending breaches and creating avenues to a future shared by the wronged and the wrongdoers.

Whether by way of a museum exhibit on American Indian

boarding schools or a book on the genocide of American Indians, the study of a traumatic past is a means to restorative justice as an end.[51] These public artifacts are a kind of collective *working through*, a critical historiography that seeks to build or rebuild a sense of community.[52] Such projects should share at least three common features. They should be *multivocal* without eschewing truth. Incorporating many voices and perspectives means approaching truth from multiple standpoints instead of one privileged position, such as that of the state or the ivory tower. History is not constructed through a celebratory multivocality but a critical multivocality that constantly questions received truths. These projects are also *dialogical* in that they cultivate an exchange of knowledge, experiences, and opinions. As noted, establishing dialogue that is open, voluntary, and evenhanded seems the most obvious way of creating affirmative interaction among disparate peoples. A third major feature is the projects' intensely *historical* approach. That is, these endeavors are distinctly diachronic, examining change through time from the distant past to the social and political present. They connect micro-truths to macro-truths and link individual stories to larger structures of power.

I hope that this book, which enters the discussion about the Camp Grant Massacre at neither its beginning nor its end, is read in the spirit of dialogue, an ongoing conversation acutely concerned with how the past shapes contemporary identities, how understanding past wrongs may lead to new remedies, and how revealing truth advances justice. I hope that readers will put down this book thinking about how our collective past is known, remembered, and forgotten. I hope that readers will look beyond the seemingly natural and inevitable modern landscape to its rich and complex local history. I hope that readers will talk with their neighbors—native and non-native alike—about the legacies of colonialism that have shaped our world through violence. I hope that readers will think about these stories the next time they open a newspaper to a story about a local dispute over water rights or Indian gaming or even events in some distant place where people are suffering unjustly. I hope that thinking about past worlds differently encourages people to think anew about their world today.

In closing, I offer one final example of an important project that has implemented many of these ideals. In 1869 the U.S. government established Fort Apache in central Arizona to control and subjugate Apache peoples.[53] Today, the fort is still standing, largely due to the White Mountain Apache Tribe's commitment to preserve and use it. The dedication of tribal members is gradually transforming this powerful symbol of American domination into a place of reconciliation. On May 20, 2000, the first annual Fort Apache Heritage Reunion was attended by more than four thousand people. The event began with a procession of different tribes, followed by government officials and community leaders. There were songs, dances, and nonviolent historical reenactments. Different reconciliation programs were offered, notably "listening posts," where attendees could share feelings and remembrances. As the organizers noted, "The objective was to encourage Apaches and non-Apaches to confront their ambiguous, even hostile, sentiments and to think about the relationship between memories, emotions, and the future."[54] Ambitious and optimistic, the White Mountain Apache Tribe's project is converting "a symbol of oppression and cultural erosion into a powerful symbol of hope, power, and self-determination."[55] Only time will tell if this project achieves its goals of explaining Apache heritage to outsiders, perpetuating Apache heritage for tribal members, and maintaining a forum that honors Apache survival. But whatever the fate of Fort Apache, the White Mountain Apache Tribe is taking social action that publicly demonstrates how to seek a balance between grief and acquiescence.

The Shore and the Sea

"Of course, one does not forget everything. But neither does one remember everything," the anthropologist Marc Augé has written. "Remembering or forgetting is doing gardener's work, selecting, pruning. Memories are like plants: there are those that need to be quickly eliminated in order to help the others burgeon, transform, flower."[56] Although when we think of memory we often focus on remembering, Augé reminds us that the other salient aspect of memory is forgetting—oblivion, "the loss of remembrance."[57] Forgetting is important because a psyche that flawlessly recalls every sensation—every whisper and song, every face and building, every embrace and touch—is a mind paralyzed by its own awareness. Thus, to order existence and to make sense of the world, an individual's consciousness paradoxically must forget to remember. "Memories are crafted by oblivion as the outlines of the shore are created by the sea," Augé poetically concludes.[58]

Marcel Proust's famous exploration of time describes a similar phenomenon. "We relive our past years not in their continuous sequence, day by day," Proust affirmed, "but in a memory focused upon the coolness or sunshine of some morning or afternoon." And between these fleeting scenes is the abeyance of memory, "vast stretches of oblivion."[59] We do not recall every event exactly as and when it occurred. Rather, our memories tend to focus on particular occurrences, experiences, and feelings that are suspended between great voids of nothingness.

A collective memory, the recollection of past events shared by a community, is no different. Tucson's myth of origin does not comprise the totality of incidents and experiences but offers a selective remembrance of things past. The names of the city founders etched into local monuments are meant to honor that part of their lives that contributed to the beginning of our home. We gain much from this—a sense of self, kinship, and belonging. Yet, we lose something when they are ennobled only as names that grace buildings, street signs, and hilltops, when we forget who these namesakes were and what they did.

Many of the descendants of the massacre's victims, as elder Philip Cassadore said, want the Camp Grant Massacre to "live forever in the memory of the Apache people." For those in Tucson and beyond it who are not Apache, I hope that the massacre also forms the shore of our memory, a shared remembrance of these events that have shaped our world. But a collective memory by its nature depends on the community as a whole. I cannot say what the makings and meanings of the massacre will be in the years ahead. I cannot say whether generations from now the massacre at Camp Grant will be remembered, a memorial to our collective past, or somehow mislaid, lost in the shadows of time. Whether and how the massacre is remembered depends on those who read this book, on those who travel the San Pedro Valley, on those who hike Wasson Peak—on those haunted by this phantom history.

Notes

Abbreviations Used in the Notes

AHF	Arizona Historical Foundation, Tempe
AHS	Arizona Historical Society, Tucson
ASM	Arizona State Museum, Tucson
BLM	Bureau of Land Management, Phoenix and Safford
NARA	National Archives and Record Administration, Washington, D.C.
NARA-PR	National Archives and Record Administration, Pacific Region, Laguna Niguel
UA	University of Arizona Library Special Collections, Tucson

Chapter 1. Phantom History

1. On the notion of "official" history, see Welch et al., "Retracing the Battle of Cibecue."

2. Climo and Cattell, *Social Memory and History*; Kaye, *The Powers of the Past*; Rosenzweig and Thalen, *The Presence of the Past*.

3. Plumb, *The Death of the Past*; Thomas, *Skull Wars*; Wallace, *Mickey Mouse History*; Zerubavel, *Recovered Roots*.

4. Sahlins, *Historical Metaphors and Mythical Realities*.

5. Appadurai, "The Past as a Scarce Resource"; Olwig, "The Burden of Heritage"; Yelvington, "History, Memory and Identity."

6. Cushing, *Zuni*.

7. Lowie, "Oral Tradition and History," 598.

8. Spinden, "Myths of the Nez Perce Indians," 158.

9. Lowie, "Oral Tradition and History," 599; emphasis in original.

10. See Whiteley, "Archaeology and Oral Tradition," 406.

11. Vansina, *Oral Tradition as History*, xii; see also Vansina, *Oral Tradition*.

12. White, *Metahistory*.

13. Whiteley, "Archaeology and Oral Tradition," 407; emphasis in original.

14. Jacobs, "The Indian and the Frontier in American History," 43.

15. Franklin, "Cultural Resource Stewardship."

16. Heider, "The Rashomon Effect."

17. Rhoades, "The 'Rashomon Effect' Reconsidered."

18. Jackson, "Storytelling Events," 372.

19. Goodwin, *Like a Brother*.

20. Ferguson and Colwell-Chanthaphonh, *History Is in the Land*.

21. I use the terms *Anglo-Americans* and *Mexican Americans* to refer to groups of people who identified themselves in the 1800s along these ethnic and national lines. I do not use *Apache Americans* or *Tohono O'odham Americans* because most American Indians were not legal citizens of the United States until 1924, a date well beyond the focus of this work.

22. Bakhtin, *Problems of Dostoevsky's Poetics*, 18.

23. Fontana, "American Indian Oral History," 367.

24. Basso, *Wisdom Sits in Places*; Silko, *Yellow Woman and a Beauty of Spirit*, 32; Smith, *Decolonizing Methodologies*, 28.

25. Wiget, "Truth and the Hopi," 197.

26. Hoffman, "Reliability and Validity in Oral History"; Wiget, "Recovering the Remembered Past"; Whiteley, "Archaeology and Oral Tradition."

27. Churchill, *Indians Are Us?* 40.

28. Dobyns, "An Appraisal of Techniques with a New Hemispheric Estimate"; Driver, "On the Population Nadir of Indians in the United States;" Jacobs, "The Tip of the Iceberg."

29. Adams, *Education for Extinction*; DeJong, "Forced to Abandon Their Farms"; Hart, *Pedro Pino*; Lomawaima, "Domesticity in the Federal Indian Schools"; Spicer, *Cycles of Conquest*; Tinker, *Missionary Conquest*; Trafzer, *The Kit Carson Campaign*.

30. Barringer and Flynn, *Colonialism and the Object*; Simpson, *Making Representations*.

31. See Mieder, "'The Only Good Indian Is a Dead Indian.'"

32. Brown, *Bury My Heart at Wounded Knee*; Cutler, *The Massacre at Sand Creek*; Fleisher, *The Bear River Massacre*.

33. Quoted in Churchill, *A Little Matter of Genocide*, 245.

34. Churchill, *A Little Matter of Genocide*; Freeman, "Puritans and Pequots"; Friedberg, "Dare to Compare"; Stannard, *American Holocaust*; Todorov, *The*

Conquest of America. On the original definition of genocide, see Lemkin, *Axis Rule in Occupied Europe,* 79–95.

35. Delano, "Report of the Commissioner of Indian Affairs," 9.

36. Roosevelt, *The Winning of the West,* 3:47–48.

37. Basso, *Western Apache Raiding and Warfare.*

38. Quoted in Ogle, *Federal Control of the Western Apaches,* 60.

39. See Scheper-Hughes and Bourgois, "Making Sense of Violence."

40. Bourguignon, "Memory in an Amnesic World," 65.

41. Bourguignon, "Memory in an Amnesic World," 66.

42. Quoted in Rylko-Bauer, "Lessons about Humanity and Survival," 38.

Chapter 2. Traditional History

1. Clum, "Es-kin-in-zin" (1928); Clum, "Es-kin-in-zin" (1929).

2. *Haské bahnzin's* name has been variously recorded as, for example, Eskin-in-zin, Eskiminzin, Hackíbanzin, or Eskiminzine. For the sake of consistency, I use the spelling provided to me by Jeanette Cassa, which is similar to Grenville Goodwin's spelling (*hàckí bánzín*); see Goodwin, *The Social Organization of the Western Apache.*

3. For example, Alexander, "Massacre at Camp Grant,"; Richard Alonzo, "Camp Grant Massacre," http://www.homepages.tesco net~richard.alonzo/ Events/campgrant.html (accessed 2003); Arnold, *The Camp Grant Massacre*; Auerbach, "Preemptive Strike Targeted Aravaipa Canyon"; Banks, "Unfriendly Fire"; Barney, "The Camp Grant Massacre"; Hammond, *The Camp Grant Massacre*; Hastings, "The Tragedy at Camp Grant in 1871"; Kitzmiller, *Embrace the Wind*; Langellier, "Camp Grant Affair, 1871"; O'Neil, "The Camp Grant Massacre"; Schellie, *Vast Domain of Blood*; Waterfall, "Vengeance at Sunrise."

4. For example, Cargill, "The Camp Grant Massacre"; Oury, "Article on Camp Grant Massacre"; Oury, "Historical Truth"; Wasson, "Bloody Retaliation"; Whitman, "Appendix A b, No. 2"; Wood, "Reminiscences of an Arizona Pioneer."

5. For example, Browning, *Enju*; Robinson, *Apache Voices*; Wilson, "Camp Grant Massacre." Notably, Tohono O'odham narratives have similarly been ignored despite several informative accounts recorded in the early part of the twentieth century; see Thomas, "Papago Land Use," 13–15; Underhill, *A Papago Calendar Record,* 36–38.

6. See chapter 5.

7. Grenville Goodwin was the chief proponent of the term "Western Apache," which he used to label "all those Apache peoples who have lived within the present boundaries of the state of Arizona during historic times,

with the exception of the Chiricahua, Warm Springs, and allied Apache, and a small band of Apaches known as the Apaches Mansos, who lived in the vicinity of Tucson"; Goodwin, "The Social Divisions and Economic Life of the Western Apache," 55.

8. See Jacksic, "Oral History in the Americas"; Welch and Riley, "Reclaiming Land and Spirit."

9. On the historicity of oral traditions, see Brown and Vibert, *Reading beyond Words*; Cruikshank, *The Social Life of Stories*; Lyons, *Ancestral Hopi Migrations*; Mihesuah, *Natives and Academics*. On the critique of text-based historiographies, see Comaroff and Comaroff, *Ethnography and the Historical Imagination*; Kruger and Mariani, *Remaking History*; Weber, *Myth and the History of the Hispanic Southwest*.

10. Day, "Oral Tradition as Complement," 100.

11. Mason, "Archaeology and Native North American Oral Tradition."

12. Merry, "Kapi'olani at the Brink," 57.

13. Basso, *Western Apache Raiding and Warfare*.

14. Basso, "Western Apache."

15. Kessel, "The Battle of Cibecue and Its Aftermath," 124.

16. Vansina, *Oral Tradition as History*, 12–13.

17. Watt and Basso, *Don't Let the Sun Step Over You*, 303.

18. Valkenburgh, "Apache Ghosts Guard the Aravaipa." According to Jeanette Cassa, Lahn could be Lonnie Bullis, a descendent of Chiquito, an Aravaipa Apache leader who resided along Aravaipa Creek for decades.

19. Throughout this book, Apache place names are derived from multiple sources whose varied orthographies presented a unique challenge. Jeanette Cassa believes in keeping the original orthography insofar as possible to allow future scholars and Apache speakers to derive their own meanings from given words. Accordingly, I have tried to provide the original orthographies wherever possible and appropriate, e.g., the figures in this chapter and long citations. Elsewhere, I substitute Jeanette Cassa's orthographies derived from her own research and the Apache Place-Name Project.

20. Vansina, *Oral Tradition as History*, 61.

21. Basso, *Wisdom Sits in Places*, 35.

22. Goodwin divided the Western Apache into five "groups," which were further partitioned into a total of twenty bands and numerous "local groups." Goodwin, *The Social Organization of the Western Apache*, 2, 6.

23. Grenville Goodwin Papers, MS 17, box 2, folder 32, ASM.

24. Goodwin, *The Social Organization of the Western Apache*, 27.

25. Grenville Goodwin Papers, MS 17, folder 74, ASM.

26. Grenville Goodwin Papers, MS 17, box 3, folder 34, ASM.

27. Goodwin, *The Social Organization of the Western Apache*, 607.

28. See Thornton, "Anthropological Studies of Native American Place Naming."

29. Basso, *Wisdom Sits in Places*, 107.

30. Grenville Goodwin Papers, MS 17, box 3, folder 34, ASM. Jeanette Cassa explained to me that "*bija gush kaiyé* is a pet name for a light-complected girl."

31. Machula, "Tribute to Mrs. Sally Ewing Dosela"; also reprinted as Paul R. Machula, "Tribute to Mrs. Sally Ewing Dosela," http://www.geocities .com/~zybt/dosela.html (accessed June 2003).

32. Record, "Aravaipa," 38–39.

33. Vansina, *Oral Tradition as History*, 21.

34. In a letter Lieutenant Royal E. Whitman wrote to the acting assistant adjutant general on February 28, 1871, he reported: "I rationed them while here, corn or flour, beans and meat, and encouraged them to come in." RG 393, entry 1, vol. 1, Camp Grant, Arizona, Letters Sent, vol. 34, March 1869– August 1871, NARA.

35. As noted in chapter 1, Anglo-American accounts also mention gathering hay. A major general wrote in regard to the Apaches at Camp Grant: "It is worthy of remark that these Indians paid for a large part of the rations issued to them by supplying hay and wood to the military posts, that the wood and hay thus furnished cost the government much less than before paid to contractors, and that the contractors they employed and customers thus lost the profits theretofore realized. It has been suggested that this may explain the Camp Grant massacre hereafter referred to." M666, roll 44, Letters Received by the Office of the Adjutant General, Main Series, 1871–1880, 1871 Annual Reports, NARA.

36. Local resident William Hopkins Tonge, writing to the commissioner of Indian affairs a week after the massacre, noted that "the Indians at the time of the massacre being so taken by surprise and considering themselves perfectly safe with scarcely any arms, those that could get away ran for the mountains." M234, roll 4, Letters Received by the Office of Indian Affairs 1824–1880, Arizona Superintendency 1863–1880, 1870–1871, NARA.

37. Record, "Aravaipa," 546.

38. Record, "Aravaipa," 365.

39. Wallace Johnson, 1990 interview by Diana Hadley, on file at BLM, Safford.

40. Record, "Aravaipa," 379.

41. See Vansina, *Oral Tradition as History*, 53–54.

42. Captain Frank Stanwood counted 493 Apache Indians present on the Camp Grant Reservation on April 22, 1871. RG 393, entry 1, vol. 1 of 1, Camp Grant, Arizona, Letters Sent, vol. 34, March 1869–August 1871, NARA.

43. For example, John Wasson wrote, "The policy of feeding and supplying hostile Indians with arms and ammunition has brought its bloody fruits. . . . The murder of four citizens in San Pedro Valley is quite certainly the work of these 'friendlies,' and so abundant had the evidence become that they were guilty of more atrocities under this assumed peace arrangement than ever before, the patient endurance of citizens was exhausted, and so they resolved retaliation." Wasson, "Bloody Retaliation."

44. Captain Frank Stanwood wrote on May 19, 1871: "I can say, and in this my reputation as an officer is at stake, that these Indians from the [time] they first came to Camp Grant up to the time I left . . . to go on scout did not engage in any depredations upon the people of this territory." RG 393, entry 1, vol. 1 of 1, Camp Grant, Arizona, Letters Sent, vol. 34, March 1869–August 1871, NARA.

45. For example, Arnold, *The Camp Grant Massacre*, 413–414; Schellie, *Vast Domain of Blood*, 149.

46. See chapter 3.

Chapter 3. Collective Histories

1. Jackson, *A Century of Dishonor*, 29.
2. Jackson, *A Century of Dishonor*, 30; see Mathes, *Helen Hunt Jackson*.
3. McMurtry, *Oh What a Slaughter*, 59; emphasis in original.
4. Tonkin, *Narrating Our Pasts*, 2.
5. See Augé, *Oblivion*, 22.
6. Forbes, "Unknown Athapaskans."
7. Bolton, *Rim of Christendom*, 361.
8. Officer, *Hispanic Arizona, 1536–1856*, 40, 48; Thiel and Vint, "The Life and Times of Santa Cruz de Terrenate."
9. Pfefferkorn, *Sonora*, 29; Sedelmayr, *Jacobo Sedelmayr*, 101, 144.
10. Spicer, *Cycles of Conquest*, 239.
11. Goodwin, "Clans of the Western Apache"; Goodwin, "The Social Divisions and Economic Life"; Kaut, "Western Apache Clan and Phratry Organization."
12. Goodwin, *The Social Organization of the Western Apache*, 616–617.
13. Goodwin, *The Social Organization of the Western Apache*, 24.
14. Basso, *Western Apache Raiding and Warfare*; Goodwin, *The Social Organization of the Western Apache*, 54; Opler, *An Apache Life-Way*; Sweeney, *Cochise, Chiricahua Apache Chief*.
15. Ferguson et al., "Field Notes."
16. Bannon, *The Spanish Borderlands Frontier, 1513–1821*, 221.
17. Officer, *Hispanic Arizona*, 66.

18. Sauer, "A Spanish Expedition into the Arizona Apacheria."

19. See, for example, Matson and Schroeder, "Cordero's Description of the Apache."

20. McCarty, *A Frontier Documentary, 1821–1848*, 36.

21. Valkenburgh, "Apache Ghosts Guard the Aravaipa."

22. Basso, *Western Apache Raiding and Warfare*, 16.

23. McCarty, *A Frontier Documentary*, 51.

24. Thrapp, *The Conquest of Apacheria*, 6–23.

25. Stein, "Historic Trails in Arizona."

26. Record, "Extermination versus Reservation."

27. Worcester, *The Apaches*, 75.

28. RG 94, Records of the Adjutant General's Officer, 1780–1917, Records of Divisions, Military Reservation Division, early 1800s–1916, box 6, NARA.

29. Ryden and Kupel, "Warfare between Indians and Americans in Arizona."

30. See Altshuler, *Chains of Command* and *Starting with Defiance*.

31. Neary and Hoff, *Arizona Military Installations*, 37.

32. MS 881, box 1, AHS.

33. RG 94, Camp Grant, Arizona Territory, Post Medical Records, vol. 687, NARA.

34. Bourke, *On the Border with Crook*, 9.

35. Stone, "The History of Fort Grant," 8.

36. RG 393, entry 1, vol. 1, Old Camp Grant, Arizona, Letters Sent, vol. 34, Mar. 1869–Aug. 1871, NARA.

37. Chronological List of Actions, &c., with Indians From January 1, 1866 to January, 1891, Office Memoranda, Adjutant General's Office, AHF.

38. Allison Diehl generously provided the data, which I tabulated. Clearly these are rough estimates, as it is hard to imagine that the non-Apaches (really Anglo-Americans and Mexican Americans) who recorded these battles and raids could honestly or accurately count the number of Apache wounded. Also, various newspaper accounts may have been missed in this broad survey, and the newspapers surely did not record every act of violence between Apaches and non-Apaches. Nevertheless, this research gives a general sense of the levels of violence during the 1860s and 1870s.

39. Basso, *Western Apache Raiding and Warfare*, 77.

40. Basso, "Western Apache," 476.

41. Cozzens, *Explorations and Adventures in Arizona and New Mexico*, 153–154.

42. Thiel, *Beneath the Streets*, 42.

43. Sonnichsen, *Tucson*.

44. *Arizona Citizen*, December 24, 1870.

45. Record, "Aravaipa," 273.

46. *Arizona Citizen*, November 12, 1870.

47. Letter from M. C. Davidson, Special Agent, to Hon. Wm. P. Dale, Commissioner of Indian Affairs, Washington D.C., February 12, 1865; M234, roll 3, Letters Received by the Office of Indian Affairs 1824–1880, Arizona Superintendency 1863–1880, 1863–1869, NARA.

48. Underhill, *Papago Woman*, 8, 69.

49. Kilcrease, "Ninety-Five Years of History of the Papago Indians."

50. All references and quotes from *bija gush kaiyé* are from Grenville Goodwin Papers, MS 17, box 3, folder 34, ASM.

51. M234, roll 3, Letters Received by the Office of Indian Affairs 1824–1880, Arizona Superintendency 1863–1880, 1863–1869, NARA.

52. M234, roll 3, Letters Received by the Office of Indian Affairs, 1824–1880, Arizona Superintendency, 1863–1880, 1863–1869, NARA.

53. RG 393, entry 1, vol. 1, Old Camp Grant, Arizona, Letters Sent, vol. 34, Mar. 1869–Aug. 1871, NARA.

54. Whitman, "Appendix A b, No. 2," 70.

55. Grenville Goodwin Papers, MS 17, box 3, folder 34, ASM; M234, roll 5, Letters Received by the Office of Indian Affairs 1824–1880, Arizona Superintendency, 1863–1880, 1872, NARA.

56. M234, roll 4, Letters Received by the Office of Indian Affairs 1824–1880, Arizona Superintendency, 1863–1880, 1870–1871, NARA.

57. Whitman, "Appendix A b, No. 2," 70.

58. Whitman, "Appendix A b, No. 2," 69; see also Records of the U.S. Commissioner Relating to U.S. v. Sidney R. Delong, 1871, NARA-PR.

59. M234, roll 4, Letters Received by the Office of Indian Affairs 1824–1880, Arizona Superintendency, 1863–1880, 1870–1871, NARA.

60. *Arizona Citizen*, March 11, 1871.

61. *Arizona Citizen*, April 15, 1871.

62. *Arizona Citizen*, April 15, 1871.

63. Even decades after the massacre, writers continued to present the attack as justifiable revenge. For example, an article in the *Arizona Citizen* published on October 1, 1913, titled "Participant Tells Tale of the Camp Grant Massacre: Butcheries by Savages Led to Swift Reprisal by the Settlers of this Country" takes precisely this line of reasoning; see also Auerbach, "Preemptive Strike Targeted Aravaipa Canyon."

64. Robinson, "Appendix A b, No. 3," 76.

65. Records of the U.S. Commissioner Relating to U.S. v. Sidney R. Delong, 1871, NARA-PR.

66. Additionally, Lieutenant Whitman wrote, "I kept them continually under my observation, until I not only came to know the faces of all the men, but also the women and children. . . . From the first I was determined to know

not only all they had, but their hopes and intentions. For this purpose I spent hours each day with them." Whitman, "Appendix A b, No. 2," 69.

67. RG 393, entry 1, vol. 1, Old Camp Grant, Arizona, Letters Sent, vol. 34, Mar. 1869–Aug 1871, NARA.

68. *Arizona Citizen*, April 15, 1871; *Weekly Arizonan*, April 22, 1871.

69. Whitman, "Appendix A b, No. 2," 71.

70. See Oury, "Article on Camp Grant Massacre."

71. RG 393, entry 1, vol. 1, Old Camp Grant, Arizona, Letters Sent, vol. 34, Mar. 1869–Aug 1871, NARA.

72. Oury, "Historical Truth."

73. Oury, "Historical Truth."

74. Underhill, "A Papago Calendar Record," 36.

75. Thomas, "Papago Land Use," 13.

76. Oury, "Historical Truth."

77. It is still uncertain who showed up that day. Using court documents, however, we may deduce a number of other participants, such as Antonio Grijalva, Placido Sosa, Joaquin Telles, and Leuterio Acedo. Historical archaeologist J. Homer Thiel, who is currently writing a history of Tucson presidio families, provided a few biographical sketches (personal communication, 2004). Antonio Grijalva was born on November 13, 1842, in Tucson. On April 7, 1870, a year before the massacre, he lost twenty-seven head of cattle during an Apache raid. Grijalva moved to Tres Alamos on the San Pedro River in 1872, first planting beans and corn on twenty acres of land. He died at Tres Alamos on June 20, 1905, from a tumor of the liver. Placido Sosa was born in the late 1840s in Tubac, Sonora. He was married just on January 8, 1871, to Mercedes Rodriguez. By June 1880, Placido was living on the San Pedro River, working as a farmer while his wife took care of their four children. Joaquin Telles was born about 1835 in Tucson, where he lived until his death from pneumonia on March 24, 1890. He had nine children. The family homesteaded a ranch fifteen miles east of Tucson on the Pantano Wash in the 1880s. In August 1869, Apaches took four cattle valued at $150 from Joaquin. Leuterio Acedo was born in 1828 or 1829 in Tucson and was married to Wenceslada Cruz around 1860. They had seven children together. In 1870 Leuterio was a farmer, and the Acedo family was living in Tucson. He died from cerebral apoplexy on December 30, 1908, at the family home on Hospital Road in Tucson.

78. MS 881, box 2, AHS.

79. Oury, "Article on Camp Grant Massacre."

80. Underhill, "A Papago Calender Record," 36.

81. MC 666, case 308, drawer 4, AHS; emphasis in original; MC 666, case 308, drawer 4, AHS.

82. Grenville Goodwin Papers, MS 17, box 2, folder 32, ASM.

83. Record, "Aravaipa," 379.

84. Colyer, "Condition of Apache Indians," 54.

85. Wallace Johnson, 1990 interview by Diana Hadley, on file at BLM, Safford.

86. Record, "Aravaipa," 379; Grenville Goodwin Papers, MS 17, box 3, folder 34, ASM.

87. Record, "Aravaipa," 364.

88. William H. Bailey, Hayden Files, AHS. Note that Bailey's participation in the massacre is self-proclaimed and somewhat suspect because other narratives or documents to date do not verify his involvement.

89. Thomas, "Papago Land Use," 14.

90. Grenville Goodwin Papers, MS 17, box 2, folder 32, ASM.

91. Oury, "Article on Camp Grant Massacre."

92. Briesly, "Appendix A b, No. 3," 72.

93. Whitman, "Appendix A b, No. 2," 70.

94. Hughes, "As Told by the Pioneers," 73; Underhill, *Papago Indian Religion*, 192.

95. *Arizona Citizen*, May 6, 1871.

96. *Arizona Citizen*, June 3, 10, 24, July 8, September 2, 1871.

97. *Arizona Citizen*, June 24, 1871; Howard, "Report of the Brigadier General O. O. Howard," 152.

98. Quoted in *Arizona Citizen*, June 24, 1871.

99. Clum, "Es-kin-in-zin" (1928), 405.

100. Alexander, "Massacre at Camp Grant," 36; Schellie, *Vast Domain of Blood*, 189.

101. Banks, "Unfriendly Fire," 23; McClintock, *Arizona*, 199.

102. Clum, "Es-kin-in-zin" (1929), 20.

103. Grenville Goodwin Papers, MS 17, box 3, folder 34, ASM.

104. Grenville Goodwin Papers, MS 17, box 3, folder 34, ASM.

105. Colyer, "Condition of Apache Indians," 54.

106. Colyer, "Condition of Apache Indians," 55.

107. Whitman, "Appendix A b, No. 2," 71.

108. MC 666, case 308, drawer 4, AHS.

109. Reuben A. Wilbur Collection, file AZ 565, UA.

110. M234, roll 6, Letters Received by the Office of Indian Affairs 1824–1880, Arizona Superintendency, 1863–1880, 1872, NARA; see also Leopoldo Carrillo folder, Hayden Files, AHS.

111. Record, "Aravaipa," 376.

112. M234, roll 4, Letters Received by the Office of Indian Affairs 1824–1880, Arizona Superintendency, 1863–1880, 1870–1871, NARA.

113. Howard, "Report of the Brigadier General O. O. Howard," 152.

114. Contreras, biographical file, AHS.

115. Reuben A. Wilbur Collection, File AZ 565, UA.

116. Underhill, "A Papago Calendar Record," 36.

117. MS 134, Cargill File, AHS.

118. *Arizona Citizen*, October 28, 1871.

119. Cargill, "The Camp Grant Massacre," 78.

120. MC 666, case 308, drawer 4, AHS. Notably, the jury consisted of John B. Allen, Granville Wheat, C. P. Rice, John Petty, M. Samenjago, Ferd Berthold, George Cox, J. Schaublin, B. W. Regan, Estevan Remades, John Montgomery, and Samuel B. Wise, many of whom had clear personal or business relationships with the accused. *Arizona Citizen*, December 9, 1871.

121. *Arizona Citizen*, December 16, 1871; *Daily Alta California*, February 3, 1872; Records of the U.S. Commissioner Relating to U.S. v. Sidney R. Delong, 1871, NARA-PR.

122. Goldberg, "As Told by Pioneers," 81.

123. Inventory and Assessment of Human Remains Potentially Related to the Apache and Yavapai Tribes in the National Museum of Natural History, case report no. 91-007, by Stuart Speaker, Beverly S. Byrd, John W. Verano, and Gretchen Stromberg, April 14, 1994. Repatriation Office, National Museum of Natural History, Smithsonian Institution, Washington, D.C.

124. *Arizona Citizen*, May 25, June 1, June 8, 1871.

125. Marion, "'As Long as the Stone Lasts,'" 120.

126. Grenville Goodwin Papers, MS 17, box 3, folder 34, ASM.

127. Quoted in Clum, "Es-kin-in-zin" (1929), 13.

128. *Arizona Weekly Citizen*, March 14, 1879.

129. *Chicago Times*, September 9, 1881.

130. *Arizona Daily Star*, January 15, 1886.

131. Davis, *The Truth about Geronimo*, 64.

132. Quoted in Clum, "Es-kin-in-zin" (1929), 22.

133. San Carlos Papers, roll 2, AHS.

134. Quoted in Clum, "Es-kin-in-zin" (1929), 22.

135. Spicer, *Cycles of Conquest*, 253.

136. RG 393, entry 1, vol. 1, Old Camp Grant, Arizona, Letters Sent, vol. 34, Mar. 1869–Aug 1871, NARA.

137. Tiffany, "San Carlos" (1880) 5.

138. Tiffany, "San Carlos" (1881).

139. *Chicago Times*, September 9, 1881.

140. Meyer, "San Carlos."

141. Perry, *Apache Reservation*, 154.

142. Perry, *Apache Reservation*, 155.

143. Bufkin, *Historical Atlas of Arizona*, 44; Hadley et al., "Environmental Change in Aravaipa."

144. Perry, *Apache Reservation*, 155.

145. Hadley et al., "Environmental Change in Aravaipa," 81.

146. Robinson, "Appendix A b, No. 3," 75.

147. Elliott, "An Indian Reservation under General George Crook"; MS 707, San Carlos Agency Records 1896–1930, box 6, folder 134, AHS.

148. The entire exchange in the following paragraphs is from MS 707, San Carlos Agency Records 1896–1930, box 6, folder 134, AHS.

149. Captain Chiquito, Land Entry Files, NARA.

150. Della Stelle with Veronica Belvado, 1990 interview by Diana Hadley, on file at BLM, Safford.

151. Goodwin, *The Social Organization of the Western Apache*, 156; McCarty, *A Frontier Documentary*, 40.

152. Claridge, "Klondyke and The Aravaipa Canyon," 181.

153. See also Claridge, "We Tried to Stay Refined," 417; Martin, *Songs My Mother Sang To Me*, 157.

154. Ferguson and Colwell-Chanthaphonh, *History Is in the Land*, 219. See also Wallace Johnson, 1990 interview by Diana Hadley, on file at BLM, Safford.

155. Colwell-Chanthaphonh, "Signs in Place," 15.

156. Basso, *Wisdom Sits in Places*, 6.

157. Ferguson and Colwell-Chanthaphonh, *History Is in the Land*, 220; Goodwin Papers MS 17, box 2, folders 26–32, ASM.

158. Record, "Aravaipa," 275.

159. Bowden, "Apaches Honor the Memory of Massacre Victims," 3C.

Chapter 4. The Historical Imagination

1. Vaughn, *The Vital Past*.

2. Thomas, "Alejandro Mayta in Fiji," 298.

3. Kammen, *Mystic Chords of Memory*; Linenthal and Engelhardt, *History Wars*; Schmidt and Patterson, *Making Alternative Histories*.

4. Lowenthal, *The Past Is a Foreign Country*, 213.

5. Echo-Hawk, "Ancient History in the New World."

6. White, *Metahistory*.

7. Appadurai, "The Past as a Scarce Resource."

8. The first published reference to the phrase "Camp Grant Massacre" is found in the *Arizona Citizen* on June 3, 1871, but as previously noted, before the attack itself, on April 29, 1871, Captain Dunn at Fort Lowell wrote a warning that called the attack a "massacre" before it even transpired; see U.S. Army, Correspondence Concerning the Camp Grant Massacre, 1871, AHS.

9. While Apache narratives are certainly textual, they are excluded from the analysis in this chapter, whose focus is Western non-Apache literature that has been available to scholars and the public.

10. The Society of Arizona Pioneers was the forerunner of the AHS; see Colwell-Chanthaphonh, "When History is Myth," 115.

11. See Coclanis, "History by the Numbers"; Herbst, *Numbered Voices*; Huff, *How to Lie with Statistics*; Urla, "Cultural Politics in an Age of Statistics."

12. While conducting psychoanalyses of authors to reveal their personal motives for selecting certain facts and not others is usually untenable and often undesirable, the selective use of historical data may be investigated through a study of the *effects* of written texts on the reader, the responses a given work of literature elicits from its audience. A textual analysis of historical prose is thus a study of the way in which the discourse of authors simultaneously represent and sway the historical imagination. Texts may be marked by *locus desperatus* (passages that are flawed or defy interpretation), and problems of validation can plague textual analysis as a method. Nevertheless, this kind of discourse analysis does not focus on just any impression of a text but an individual analytical reading of it. Textual analyses, which are based on logical explanations of and responses to visible changes and asymmetries in texts, are more rigorous than examinations of, for example, an impressionistic response to a Van Gogh landscape, an often personal and idiosyncratic reaction. A critic working within this analytical framework could not legitimately tell me that my fondness for Van Gogh is incorrect. I could be informed, however, that the given data do not support my analytical interpretations. Thus, distinctions can be made between singular emotional reactions and generalizable claims built from evidentiary criteria. Accordingly, textual analyses link data presented in the texts themselves to the analyst's interpretation in an effort to move beyond personal and idiosyncratic opinion. See Bernard and Ryan, "Text analysis" and Eco, *The Limits of Interpretation* for a more extensive discussion of this method and related issues.

13. In order to systematically quantify these data, several approaches were taken. When reporting empirical data, several authors would use language such as "between 10 and 30 children were captured." In these cases, I took an average of the two numbers—in this example, it would be 20—on the assumption that a reader might suppose the mean to be an approximation of the truth. Other authors would refer to numerical data without employing specific numbers. For instance, "a mob left Tucson," or "a few escaped." In these cases, references were not quantified. Finally, authors often modified numbers with qualifiers such as "approximately," "almost," and "nearly." In these cases, I used the number without the qualifier on the assumption that the general reader would gloss over the qualifier and more likely recall the number itself. This approach is appropriate to the overall study in this chapter, which aims to understand not so much the complex intended meanings of the authors but the effects of their writings.

14. U.S. Army, Correspondence Concerning the Camp Grant Massacre, 1871, AHS.

15. *Arizona Citizen*, June 10, 1871.

16. The *Arizona Citizen* claimed the number of killed was 85 and "not less than 85" on May 6 and June 3, 1871, respectively. The *Arizona Miner* varied more, putting the number of murdered at 125 (May 5, 1871), 123 to 125 (May 27, 1871), and 85 (June 3, 1871). Notably, two later *Arizona Miner* articles that attempted to mount a defense for the attackers, "The Camp Grant Massacre" (June 10, 1871) and "The Alleged Arizona Massacre" (July 8, 1871), do not even mention the number killed.

17. *Arizona Miner*, May 27, 1871.

18. www.u.arizona.edu/~eryn/camp_grant.htm (accessed January 2003).

19. Reuben A. Wilbur Collection, UA.

20. *Arizona Citizen*, May 6, 1871; *Arizona Miner*, May 27, June 3, 1871.

21. Clum, *Annual Report of the Commissioner of Indian Affairs*, 69; see also Clum, *Apache Agent*, 85.

22. Marion, "'As Long as the Stone Lasts,'" 120.

23. For example, Anderson, *Imagined Communities*.

24. *Arizona Miner*, July 8, 1871; Hughes, "As Told by the Pioneers"; Wood, "Reminiscences of an Arizona Pioneer."

25. Peter Vokac, "The Camp Grant Massacre as Tucson Residents Saw It in 1871," http://www.azstarnet.com/public/comm_editorials/Peter_Vokac_334394.html (accessed April 2002).

26. Oury, "Historical Truth."

27. Oury, "Article on Camp Grant Massacre," 8.

28. Oury, "Article on Camp Grant Massacre," 9.

29. Hughes, "As Told by the Pioneers," 72.

30. *Daily Alta California*, February 3, 1872.

31. *Daily Alta California*, February 3, 1872.

32. See Record, "Extermination versus Reservation," 149–159.

33. Albert S. Reynolds, Papers, 1926–1936, AHS.

34. William H. Bailey, Hayden Files, AHS.

35. Record, "Aravaipa," 342; Records of the U.S. Commissioner Relating to U.S. v. Sidney R. Delong, 1871, NARA-PR.

36. Record, "Aravaipa," 327.

37. Kane, "An Honorable and Upright Man."

38. Berkhofer, *The White Man's Indian*, 28.

39. O'Neil, "The Camp Grant Massacre," 24.

40. Arnold, *The Camp Grant Massacre*, 352.

41. Arnold, *The Camp Grant Massacre*, 404.

42. Russell, "How Many Indians Were Killed?" 45.

43. Arnold, *The Camp Grant Massacre*, 413–414; Schellie, *Vast Domain of Blood*, 149.

44. Briesly, "Appendix A b, No. 3," 72.

45. William H. Bailey, Hayden Files, AHS.

46. Goodwin Papers, MS 17, box 2, folder 32, ASM.

47. Lowenthal, *The Past Is a Foreign Country*, 214–219.

48. Lowenthal, *The Past Is a Foreign Country*, 218.

49. Thomas, "Alejandro Mayta in Fiji," 303.

Chapter 5. History, Memory, Justice

1. Bowden, "Apaches Honor the Memory of Massacre Victims," 3C; see also Marquez, "Apache Massacre at Camp Grant Recalled."

2. Bowden, "Apaches Honor the Memory of Massacre Victims," 1C.

3. Bowden, "Apaches Honor the Memory of Massacre Victims," 3C.

4. Ferguson et al., "Field Notes."

5. Record, "Aravaipa," 379.

6. Ferguson et al., "Field Notes."

7. See Welch, "White Eyes' Lies and the Battle for Dził Nchaa Si'an," 100.

8. Allen, "Camp Grant Remembered," 10A and "Kin Want Death Site Marked."

9. Volante, "Massacred Apaches Commemorated," 1A.

10. Volante, "Massacred Apaches Commemorated," 1A.

11. Bowden, "Apaches Honor the Memory of Massacre Victims," 3C.

12. Jackson, "Storytelling Events," 357.

13. Jackson, "Storytelling Events," 367.

14. Jackson, "Storytelling Events," 370.

15. Jackson, "Storytelling Events," 370.

16. Bourdieu, *Pascalian Meditations*, 223; see also Jackson, "Storytelling Events," 370.

17. Cited in Vaughn, "History," 4.

18. Momaday, *The Names*, 97.

19. Point, "Foreword," xiv.

20. Zinn, "What is Radical History?" 168.

21. Gourevitch, *We Wish to Inform You.*

22. Zinn, "What is Radical History?" 168–169.

23. Waldron, "Superseding Historical Injustice."

24. Waldron, "Superseding Historical Injustice," 27.

25. Lyons, "The New Indian Claims and Original Rights to Land."

26. Sher, "Ancient Wrongs and Modern Rights," 17.

27. Howard-Hassman, "Getting to Reparations."

28. See Biondi, "The Rise of the Reparations Movement."

29. Minow, "The Hope for Healing," 238.

30. See Arendt, "From Eichmann in Jerusalem," 99; Weissmark, *Justice Matters*, 6.

31. Kaplan, *Conscience and Memory*, x.

32. Tutu, *No Future Without Forgiveness*, 15–54.

33. Scheper-Hughes and Bourgois, "Making Sense of Violence," 27.

34. Asmal et al., *Reconciliation Through Truth*, 14; Tutu, *No Future Without Forgiveness*, 54–55.

35. Phelps, *Shattered Voices*, 123.

36. Levi, *The Drowned and the Saved*, 13.

37. Rotberg, "Truth Commissions," 6.

38. Eze, "Transition and the Reasons of Memory," 756.

39. Krog, *Country of My Skull*, 76; see Meredith, *Coming to Terms*.

40. Mamdani, "Amnesty or Impunity?" 42.

41. Chapman and Ball, "The Truth of Truth Commissions," 7.

42. Flournoy and Pan, "Dealing with Demons," 111.

43. Chapman and Ball, "The Truth of Truth Commissions," 41.

44. Howard-Hassman, "Getting to Reparations," 826.

45. Robben, "How Traumatized Societies Remember," 122.

46. Levi, *The Drowned and the Saved*, 42, 48, 56.

47. See Hinton, "Why Did You Kill?" 118. The source for Whitman's statement is cited in chapter 3, note 53. The source for the statement about Carrillo and Romero is cited in chapter 3, note 110.

48. Farmer, "The Banality of Agency," 133.

49. See Yoneyama, "Traveling Memories, Contagious Justice," 61.

50. Kelsall, "Truth, Lies, Ritual."

51. See, for example, Hoerig, "Remembering Our Indian School Days."

52. LaCapra, *Writing History, Writing Trauma*, 65.

53. Goodwin, *The Social Organization of the Western Apache*, 22.

54. Welch and Riley, "Reclaiming Land and Spirit," 10–11.

55. Welch and Riley, "Reclaiming Land and Spirit," 10.

56. Augé, *Oblivion*, 17.

57. Augé, *Oblivion*, 16.

58. Augé, *Oblivion*, 20.

59. Proust, *In Search of Lost Time*, 544.

Glossary

agave. A desert plant, also commonly referred to as mescal, that grows throughout southern Arizona. The agave heart is gathered, roasted, and processed, and it is a vital food item for Apaches.

Akimel O'odham. Historically Pima, a Native American group closely related to the Tohono O'odham who today live in southern Arizona.

Aravaipa band. A Western Apache band known in Apache as *tcéjìné* (Dark Rocks People), named after a place called *tséijìn* (Dark Rocks) in Aravaipa Canyon.

Aravaipa Canyon. A watershed between the Gila and San Pedro river valleys in southern Arizona. Home to several Apache bands, including the Aravaipa and Pinal bands.

Big Sycamore Stands There. A place-name, *gashdla'á cho o'aa* in Apache. A traditional place to live, farm, and gather along Aravaipa Creek, this is the spot where the Camp Grant Massacre occurred.

bija gush kaiyé. An Apache woman interviewed about the massacre by Grenville Goodwin in the 1930s. Jeanette Cassa has noted that *bija gush kaiyé* is a pet name for a light-complected girl.

Briesly, Conant B. Acting assistant surgeon of the United States Army at Camp Grant when the massacre occurred.

Camp Grant. A military post at the confluence of the San Pedro River and Aravaipa Creek. Established in 1860 under the name Fort Aravaypa, it was also called Fort Breckinridge and Fort Stanford before being named Camp Grant in 1865. This installation should not be confused with Fort Grant, a post farther east on Aravaipa Creek established after Camp Grant was dismantled in 1872.

Carrillo, Leopoldo. A prominent Tucson businessman who took a ten-year-old captive girl named Lola following the massacre.

Cassa, Jeanette. A San Carlos Apache elder who assisted this book's research and a steward of vast knowledge of Apache history and traditions.

Chiquito. An Apache leader who survived the massacre and later lived at Big Sycamore Stands There. Land along Aravaipa Creek was allotted to him. Also known as Captain Chiquito, he later changed his name to Bullis.

Chiricahua Apache. A group of Apache peoples living in southern Arizona and western New Mexico, culturally and politically distinct from the Western Apache.

Clum, John P. An Indian agent at San Carlos between 1874 and 1877. Later he was an important advocate for *haské bahnzin*.

Colyer, Vincent. An Indian commissioner under President Grant charged with seeking peace between Indian groups and American settlers. He spoke with Apache leaders in the fall of 1871 after the massacre.

Curley, Sherman. An Apache elder interviewed by Grenville Goodwin in the 1930s. Also known as *m-ba-lse-śla* in Apache.

DeLong, Sidney R. A participant in the massacre and the lead defendant in the subsequent trial in December 1871. He became mayor of Tucson in 1872.

Dudleyville. A small farming and mining community in the northern end of the San Pedro Valley.

Elías, Jesús María. A participant in the massacre and the ringleader of the Mexican American participants. He was a prominent Mexican American businessman in Tucson.

Eskiminzin. See *haské bahnzin*.

genocide. A term coined by Raphaël Lemkin in 1944 from the Greek *genos*, meaning race or kind, and the Latin *cide*, to kill. It was originally defined as including a composite of different acts of persecution and destruction.

Gila River Valley. A watershed in southern Arizona important to numerous Apache groups. The San Pedro River flows into the Gila River.

Goodwin, Grenville. A renowned anthropologist who recorded many traditions among the Western Apache in the 1930s. Goodwin died suddenly in 1940, leaving much of his work unpublished.

gashdla'á cho o'aa. See Big Sycamore Stands There.

haské bahnzin. An Aravaipa Apache leader during the events surrounding the massacre. His name translates as "anger stands beside him." Also known as Eskiminzin, Hosh-baî-ban-zîn, Es-cim-en-zeen, Eskemazine, and other variations.

Hooke, Walter. An Apache elder who belonged to the Aravaipa band. Also known as *hosh-ke-nes-tz-oot* in Apache, he was interviewed by Grenville Goodwin in the 1930s.

Howard, Oliver Otis. A Civil War veteran and major general who came to

Arizona in 1872 to try to establish peace among the settlers, soldiers, and various Indian groups.

Hughes, Samuel. The adjutant general of Arizona at the time of the massacre. He furnished guns and provisions for the attackers.

kowa. Often referred to as a wickiup, a small brush and wood structure built by Apaches.

Lahn. An Apache elder interviewed by Richard van Valkenburgh in the 1940s.

lednłii. An Apache place-name (Flows Together) for the confluence of the San Pedro River and Aravaipa Creek. This is the site of Camp Grant.

mescal. See agave.

Oury, William S. A prominent Tucson participant in the massacre and the ringleader of its Anglo-American participants.

Papago. See Tohono O'odham.

Pima. See Akimel O'odham.

Pinal band. *'tis'évàn,* named after *'tìsévà* (Cottonwoods In Gray Wedge Shape). They lived mostly in the area just north of the Gila River.

Rillito River. A small wash that runs through Tucson and the meeting spot for the attackers.

Romero, Francisco. A prominent Tucsonan who took two captive Apache children following the massacre.

sáikiné. Sand House People, an Apache term used to describe the Tohono O'odham (Papago), Akimel O'odham (Pima), ancient tribes in general, and possibly the Sobaipuri Indians who lived in the San Pedro Valley until the mid-eighteenth century.

San Carlos. A town in eastern Arizona on the San Carlos Apache Reservation, established along the Gila River.

San Carlos Apache. One of Goodwin's five distinct groups of the Western Apache, with four bands: Pinal, Aravaipa, San Carlos, and Apache Peaks. The term is used generally to describe the Apache people living on the San Carlos Apache Reservation in eastern Arizona.

San Pedro River Valley. A watershed in southern Arizona, beginning in Mexico and stretching 140 miles northward until it reaches the Gila River.

Santa Cruz River Valley. A watershed in southern Arizona just west of the San Pedro Valley and an important source of water for early Tucsonans.

Sobaipuri. A group of Native Americans who lived in the San Pedro Valley until the mid-eighteenthth century. They were the ancestors of the Tohono O'odham.

Stoneman, George. A United States Army general and commander of the Department of Arizona during the events of the massacre.

tcéjìné. See Aravaipa band.

Tohono O'odham. A large Native American tribe in southern Arizona, historically called the Papago.

Tonge, William. A resident near Camp Grant at the time of the massacre who was sympathetic to the Apache victims.

Wasson, John. Editor of Tucson's territorial-era newspaper the *Arizona Citizen*.

Western Apache. A group of Apache peoples defined by Grenville Goodwin, among others, as the Apache communities with shared cultural traits living in eastern and southern Arizona. Goodwin divided the Western Apache into five groups (Northern Tonto, Southern Tonto, Cibecue, White Mountain, and San Carlos), which were further partitioned into twenty bands and numerous local groups.

White Mountain Apache. One of Goodwin's five distinct groups of the Western Apache, divided into the Eastern White Mountain band and the Western White Mountain band. The term is used generally to describe the Apache people living on the White Mountain Apache Reservation in eastern Arizona.

Whitman, Royal E. The United States Army lieutenant in charge of Camp Grant in early 1871.

Wilbur, Reuben A. An Indian agent of the Tohono O'odham (then called the Papago) during the events of the massacre.

Works Cited

Adams, David Wallace. *Education for Extinction: American Indians and the Boarding School Experience, 1875–1928*. Lawrence: University Press of Kansas, 1997.

Alexander, J. C. "Massacre at Camp Grant." *Mankind* 1, no. 11 (1969): 34–40.

Allen, Paul L. "Camp Grant Remembered." *Tucson Citizen*, April 3, 1995, 10A.

———. "Kin Want Death Site Marked." *Tucson Citizen*, April 3, 1995, 1A, 10A.

Altshuler, Constance Wynn. *Chains of Command: Arizona and the Army, 1856–1875*. Tucson: Arizona Historical Society, 1981.

———. *Starting with Defiance: Nineteenth Century Arizona Military Posts*. Tucson: Arizona Historical Society, 1983.

Anderson, Benedict. *Imagined Communities: Reflections on the Origins and Spread of Nationalism*. London: Verso, 1983.

Appadurai, Arjun. "The Past as a Scarce Resource." *Man*, new ser., 16, no. 2 (1981): 201–219.

Arendt, Hannah. "From Eichmann in Jerusalem: A Report on the Banality of Evil." In *Violence in War and Peace*, edited by Nancy Scheper-Hughes and Philippe Bourgois, 91–100. Oxford: Blackwell, 2004.

Arnold, Elliott. *The Camp Grant Massacre*. New York: Simon and Schuster, 1976.

Asmal, Kader, Louise Asmal, and Ronald Suresh Roberts. *Reconciliation through Truth: A Reckoning of Apartheid's Criminal Governance*. Cape Town: David Philip Publishers, 1997.

Auerbach, Evaline Jones. "Preemptive Strike Targeted Aravaipa Canyon." *The Oracle* 5, no. 3 (2003): 16.

Augé, Marc. *Oblivion*. Minneapolis: University of Minnesota Press, 2004.

Bakhtin, Mikhail. *Problems of Dostoevsky's Poetics*. Minneapolis: University of Minnesota Press, 1984.

Banks, Leo W. "Unfriendly Fire: The Killing of a Farmer by an Apache Chief Speaks Volumes about the Desperate Times of 1871." *Arizona Highways*, June 2002, 20–23.

Bannon, John Francis. *The Spanish Borderlands Frontier, 1513–1821*. New York: Holt, Rinehart, and Winston, 1970.

Barney, James M. "The Camp Grant Massacre." *The Sheriff*, March 1946, 89–101.

Barringer, Tim, and Tom Flynn, eds. *Colonialism and the Object: Empire, Material Culture and the Museum*. London: Routledge, 1998.

Basso, Keith H. "Western Apache." In *Handbook of North American Indians*. Vol. 10, *Southwest*, edited by Alfonso Ortiz, 462–488. Washington, D.C.: Smithsonian Institution, 1983.

———. *Western Apache Raiding and Warfare: From the Notes of Grenville Goodwin*. Tucson: University of Arizona Press, 1993.

———. *Wisdom Sits in Places: Landscape and Language among the Western Apache*. Albuquerque: University of New Mexico Press, 1996.

Berkhofer, Robert F. *The White Man's Indian: Images of the American Indian from Columbus to the Present*. New York: Vintage Books, 1978.

Bernard, H. Russell, and Gery W. Ryan. "Text Analysis: Qualitative and Quantitative Methods." In *Handbook of Methods in Cultural Anthropology*, edited by H. Russell Bernard, 595–646. Walnut Creek, Calif.: AltaMira Press, 1998.

Biondi, Martha. "The Rise of the Reparations Movement." *Radical History Review* 87 (Fall 2003): 5–18.

Bolton, Herbert Eugene. *Rim of Christendom: A Biography of Eusebio Francisco Kino, Pacific Coast Pioneer*. New York: MacMillan, 1936.

Bourdieu, Pierre. *Pascalian Meditations*. Cambridge: Polity Press, 2000.

Bourguignon, Erika. "Memory in an Amnesic World: Holocaust, Exile, and the Return of the Suppressed." *Anthropological Quarterly* 78, no. 1 (2005): 63–88.

Bourke, John G. *On the Border with Crook*. Lincoln: University of Nebraska Press, 1971.

Bowden, Charles. "Apaches Honor the Memory of Massacre Victims." *Tucson Citizen*, April 30, 1984, 1C, 3C.

Briesly, Conant B. "Appendix A b, No. 3." In *Annual Report of the Commissioner of Indian Affairs to the Secretary of the Interior for the Year 1871*, 71–72. Washington, D.C.: Government Printing Office, 1872.

Brown, Dee. *Bury My Heart at Wounded Knee: An Indian History of the American West*. New York: Henry Holt, 2001.

Brown, Jennifer S. H., and Elizabeth Vibert, eds. *Reading beyond Words: Contexts for Native History*. Peterborough, ON: Broadview Press, 1996.

Browning, Sinclair. *Enju: The Life and Struggles of an Apache Chief from the Little Running Water*. Lincoln, Nebr.: iUniverse, 2000.

Bufkin, Don. *Historical Atlas of Arizona*. Norman: University of Oklahoma Press, 1986.

Cargill, Andrew Hays. "The Camp Grant Massacre: Reminiscences of Andrew Hays Cargill, 1907." *Arizona Historical Review* 7, no. 3 (1936): 73–79.

Chapman, Audrey R., and Patrick Ball. "The Truth of Truth Commissions: Comparative Lessons from Haiti, South Africa, and Guatemala." *Human Rights Quarterly* 23, no. 1 (2001): 1–43.

Churchill, Ward. *Indians Are Us? Culture and Genocide in Native North America*. Monroe, Maine: Common Courage Press, 1994.

———. *A Little Matter of Genocide: Holocaust and Denial in the Americas, 1492 to the Present*. San Francisco: City Lights Books, 1997.

Claridge, Eleanor Postle. "Klondyke and the Aravaipa Canyon." Manuscript on file, Special Collections, Cline Library, Northern Arizona University.

Claridge, Junietta. "We Tried to Stay Refined: Pioneering in the Mineral Strip." *Journal of Arizona History* 16, no. 4 (1975): 405–426.

Climo, Jacob J., and Maria G. Cattell, eds. *Social Memory and History: Anthropological Perspectives*. Walnut Creek: AltaMira Press, 2002.

Clum, H. R., ed. *Annual Report of the Commissioner of Indian Affairs to the Secretary of the Interior for the Year 1871*. Washington, D.C.: Government Printing Office, 1872.

Clum, John P. "Es-kin-in-zin." *New Mexico Historical Review* 3, no. 4 (1928): 399–420.

———. "Es-kin-in-zin." *New Mexico Historical Review* 4, no. 1 (1929): 1–27.

Clum, Woodworth. *Apache Agent: The Story of John P. Clum*. Lincoln: University of Nebraska Press, 1963.

Coclanis, Peter A. "History by the Numbers: Why Counting Matters." *OAH Magazine of History* 7, no. 2 (1992):5–8.

Colwell-Chanthaphonh, Chip. "Signs in Place: Native American Perspectives of the Past in the San Pedro Valley of Southeastern Arizona." *The Kiva* 69, no. 1 (2003): 5–29.

Colwell-Chanthaphonh, Chip. "When History Is Myth: Genocide and the Transmogrification of American Indians." *American Indian Culture and Research Journal* 29, no. 2 (2005): 113–118.

Colyer, Vincent. "Condition of Apache Indians—Camp Apache, White Mountains, Arizona." In *Annual Report of the Commissioner of Indian Affairs to the Secretary of the Interior for the Year 1871*, 50–57. Washington, D.C.: Government Printing Office, 1872.

Comaroff, John, and Jean Comaroff. *Ethnography and the Historical Imagination*. Boulder, Colo.: Westview Press, 1992.

Cozzens, Samuel Woodworth. *Explorations and Adventures in Arizona and New Mexico*. Secaucus, N.J.: Castle Press, 1988.

Cruikshank, Julie. *The Social Life of Stories: Narrative and Knowledge in the Yukon Territory*. Lincoln: University of Nebraska Press, 1998.

Cushing, Frank Hamilton. *Zuni: Selected Writings of Frank Hamilton Cushing*, edited by Jesse Green. Lincoln: University of Nebraska Press, 1979.

Cutler, Bruce. *The Massacre at Sand Creek*. Norman: University of Oklahoma Press, 1997.

Davis, Britton. *The Truth about Geronimo*. New Haven: Yale University Press, 1929.

Day, Gordon M. "Oral Tradition as Complement." *Ethnohistory* 19, no. 2 (1972): 99–108.

DeJong, David H. "Forced to Abandon Their Farms: Water Deprivation and Starvation among the Gila River Pima, 1892–1904." *American Indian Culture and Research Journal* 28, no. 3 (2004): 29–56.

Delano, Columbus. "Report of the Commissioner of Indian Affairs." In *Annual Report of the Commissioner of Indian Affairs to the Secretary of the Interior for the Year 1872*, 1–105. Washington, D.C.: Government Printing Office, 1872.

Dobyns, Henry F. "An Appraisal of Techniques with a New Hemispheric Estimate." *Current Anthropology* 7, no. 4 (1966): 395–416.

Driver, Harold E. "On the Population Nadir of Indians in the United States." *Current Anthropology* 9, no. 4 (1968): 330.

Echo-Hawk, Roger. "Ancient History in the New World: Integrating Oral Traditions and the Archaeological Record in Deep Time." *American Antiquity* 65, no. 2 (2000): 267–290.

Eco, Umberto. *The Limits of Interpretation*. Bloomington: Indiana University Press, 1990.

Elliott, Charles P. "An Indian Reservation under General George Crook." *Military Affairs* 12, no. 2 (1948): 91–102.

Eze, Emmanuel Chukwudi. "Transition and the Reasons of Memory." *South Atlantic Quarterly* 103, no. 4 (2003): 755–768.

Farmer, Paul. "The Banality of Agency: Bridging Personal Narrative and Political Economy." *Anthropological Quarterly* 78, no. 1 (2005): 125–135.

Ferguson, T. J., and Chip Colwell-Chanthaphonh. *History Is in the Land: Multivocal Tribal Traditions in Arizona's San Pedro Valley*. Tucson: University of Arizona Press, 2006.

Ferguson, T. J., and Chip Colwell-Chanthaphonh, with contributions by Roger Anyon and Patrick D. Lyons. "Field Notes of the San Pedro Ethnohistory Project." 2004. Manuscript on file, Arizona Historical Society, Tucson.

Fleisher, Kass. *The Bear River Massacre and the Making of History*. Albany: State University of New York Press, 2004.

Flournoy, Michèle, and Michael Pan. "Dealing with Demons: Justice and Reconciliation." *Washington Quarterly* 25, no. 4 (2002): 111–123.

Fontana, Bernard L. "American Indian Oral History: An Anthropologist's Note." *History and Theory* 8, no. 3 (1969): 366–370.

Forbes, Jack D. "Unknown Athapaskans: The Identification of the Jano, Jocome, Jumano, Manso, Suma, and Other Indian Tribes of the Southwest." *Ethnohistory* 6, no. 2 (1959): 97–159.

Franklin, John Hope. "Cultural Resource Stewardship." Paper presented at the National Park Service General Conference, St. Louis, 2000.

Freeman, Michael. "Puritans and Pequots: The Question of Genocide." *New England Quarterly* 68, no. 2 (1995): 278–293.

Friedberg, Lilian. "Dare to Compare: Americanizing the Holocaust." *American Indian Quarterly* 24, no. 3 (2000): 353–380.

Goldberg, Isaac. "As Told by Pioneers: Isaac Goldberg." *Arizona Historical Review* 6, no. 2 (1935): 74–82.

Goodwin, Grenville. "Clans of the Western Apache." *New Mexico Historical Review* 8, no. 3 (1933): 176–182.

———. "The Social Divisions and Economic Life of the Western Apache." *American Anthropologist* 37, no. 1 (1935): 55–64.

———. *The Social Organization of the Western Apache*. Chicago: University of Chicago Press, 1942.

Goodwin, Neil. *Like a Brother: Grenville Goodwin's Apache Years, 1928–1939*. Tucson: University of Arizona Press, 2004.

Gourevitch, Philip. *We Wish to Inform You that Tomorrow We Will Be Killed with Our Families: Stories from Rwanda*. New York: Farrar, Straus, and Giroux, 1998.

Hadley, Diana, Peter Warshall, and Don Bufkin. "Environmental Change in Aravaipa, 1870–1970: An Ethnoecological Survey." 1991. Manuscript on file, Bureau of Land Management, Safford.

Hammond, George P. *The Camp Grant Massacre: A Chapter in Apache History*. Proceedings of the Pacific Coast Branch of the American Historical Association. Berkeley, Calif., 1929.

Hart, Richard E. *Pedro Pino: Governor of Zuni Pueblo, 1830–1878*. Logan: Utah State University Press, 2003.

Hastings, James E. "The Tragedy at Camp Grant in 1871." *Arizona and the West* 1, no. 2 (1959): 146–160.

Heider, Karl G. "The Rashomon Effect: When Ethnographers Disagree." *American Anthropologist* 90, no. 1 (1988): 73–81.

Herbst, Susan. *Numbered Voices: How Opinion Polling Has Shaped American Politics*. Chicago: University of Chicago Press, 1993.

Hinton, Alexander Laban. "Why Did You Kill? The Cambodian Genocide and the Dark Side of Face and Honor." *Journal of Asian Studies* 57, no. 1 (1998): 93–122.

Hoerig, Karl A. "Remembering Our Indian School Days: The Boarding School Experience." *American Anthropologist* 104, no. 2 (2002): 642–646.

Hoffman, Alice. "Reliability and Validity in Oral History." In *Oral History: An Interdisciplinary Anthology*, edited by David K. Dunaway and Willa K. Baum, 87–93. Walnut Creek, Calif.: AltaMira Press, 1996.

Howard, Oliver O. "Report of the Brigadier General O. O. Howard, U.S.A." In *Annual Report of the Commissioner of Indian Affairs to the Secretary of the Interior for the Year 1872*, 148–158. Washington, D.C.: Government Printing Office, 1872.

Howard-Hassman, Rhoda E. "Getting to Reparations: Japanese Americans and African Americans." *Social Forces* 83, no. 2 (2004): 823–840.

Huff, Darrell. *How to Lie with Statistics*. New York: W. W. Norton, 1993.

Hughes, Atanacia Santa Cruz. "As Told by the Pioneers: Mrs. Samuel Hughes, Tucson." *Arizona Historical Review* 6 (1935): 66–74.

Jacksic, Ivan. "Oral History in the Americas." *Journal of American History* 79, no. 2 (1992): 590–600.

Jackson, Helen Hunt. *A Century of Dishonor: A Sketch of the United States Government's Dealings with Some of the Indian Tribes*. New York: Harper and Brothers, 1881.

Jackson, Michael. "Storytelling Events, Violence, and the Appearance of the Past." *Anthropological Quarterly* 78, no. 2 (2005): 355–375.

Jacobs, Wilbur R. "The Indian and the Frontier in American History: A Need for Revision." *Western Historical Quarterly* 4, no. 1 (1973): 43–56.

———. "The Tip of the Iceberg: Pre-Columbian Indian Demography and Some Implications for Revisionism." *William and Mary Quarterly*, 3d ser., 31, no. 1 (1974): 123–132.

Kammen, Michael. *Mystic Chords of Memory: The Transformation of Tradition in American Culture*. New York: Vintage Books, 1991.

Kane, Randy. "'An Honorable and Upright Man': Sidney R. DeLong as Post Trader at Fort Bowie." *Journal of Arizona History* 19, no. 3 (1978): 297–314.

Kaplan, Harold. *Conscience and Memory: Meditations in a Museum of the Holocaust*. Chicago: University of Chicago Press, 1994.

Kaut, Charles R. "Western Apache Clan and Phratry Organization." *American Anthropologist* 58, no. 1 (1956): 140–146.

Kaye, Harvey. *The Powers of the Past: Reflections on the Crisis and the Promise of History*. Minneapolis: University of Minnesota Press, 1992.

Kelsall, Tim. "Truth, Lies, Ritual: Preliminary Reflections on the Truth and

Reconciliation Commission in Sierra Leone." *Human Rights Quarterly* 27, no. 2 (2005): 361–391.

Kessel, William B. "The Battle of Cibecue and Its Aftermath: A White Mountain Apache's Account." *Ethnohistory* 21, no. 2 (1974): 123–134.

Kilcrease, A. T. "Ninety-Five Years of History of the Papago Indians." *SW Monuments Monthly Report*. April supplement (1939), 297–310.

Kitzmiller, Chelley. *Embrace the Wind*. New York: Topaz, 1997.

Krog, Antjie. *Country of My Skull*. London: Jonathan Cape, 1998.

Kruger, Barbara, and Phil Mariani, eds. *Remaking History*. Seattle: Bay Press, 1989.

LaCapra, Dominick, *Writing History, Writing Trauma*. Baltimore: Johns Hopkins University Press, 2001.

Langellier, J. Phillip. "Camp Grant Affair, 1871: Milestone in Federal Indian Policy?" *Military History of Texas and the Southwest* 15, no. 2 (1979): 17–30.

Lemkin, Raphaël. *Axis Rule in Occupied Europe*. Washington, D.C.: Carnegie Endowment for International Peace, 1944.

Levi, Primo. *The Drowned and the Saved*. New York: Vintage Books, 1988.

Linenthal, Edward T., and Tom Engelhardt. *History Wars: The Enola Gay and Other Battles for the American Past*. New York: Henry Holt, 1996.

Lomawaima, K. Tsianina. "Domesticity in the Federal Indian Schools: The Power of Authority over Mind and Body." *American Ethnologist* 20, no. 2 (1993): 227–250.

Lowenthal, David. *The Past Is a Foreign Country*. Cambridge: Cambridge University Press, 1985.

Lowie, Robert H. "Oral Tradition and History." *American Anthropologist* 17, no. 3 (1915): 597–599.

Lyons, David. "The New Indian Claims and Original Rights to Land." *Social Theory and Practice* 4, no. 3 (1977): 249–273.

Lyons, Patrick D. *Ancestral Hopi Migrations*. Tucson: University of Arizona Press, 2003.

Machula, Paul R. "Tribute to Mrs. Sally Ewing Dosela." *San Carlos Apache Moccasin*, January 14, 1997.

Mamdani, Mahmood. "Amnesty or Impunity? A Preliminary Critique of the Report of the Truth and Reconciliation Commission of South Africa (TRC)." *Diacritics* 32, nos. 3–4 (2005): 33–59.

Marion, Jeanie. "'As Long as the Stone Lasts': General O. O. Howard's 1872 Peace Conference." *Journal of Arizona History* 35, no. 2 (1994): 109–140.

Marquez, Dennis. "Apache Massacre at Camp Grant Recalled with 'Peace and Brotherhood.'" *San Manuel Miner*, May 9, 1984.

Martin, Patricia Preciado. *Songs My Mother Sang to Me: An Oral History of Mexican American Women*. Tucson: University of Arizona Press, 1992.

Mason, Ronald J. "Archaeology and Native North American Oral Tradition." *American Antiquity* 65, no. 2 (2000): 239–266.

"Massacres II." *Wild West Tech*. DVD. New York: The History Channel, 2005.

Mathes, Valerie Sherer. *Helen Hunt Jackson and Her Indian Reform Legacy*. Norman: University of Oklahoma Press, 1997.

Matson, Daniel S., and Albert H. Schroeder. "Cordero's Description of the Apache—1796." *New Mexico Historical Review* 32, no. 4 (1957): 335–356.

McCarty, Kieran, ed. *A Frontier Documentary: Sonora and Tucson, 1821–1848*. Tucson: University of Arizona Press, 1997.

McClintock, James H. *Arizona, Prehistoric, Aboriginal, Pioneer, Modern; The Nation's Youngest Commonwealth within a Land of Ancient Culture*. Chicago: S. J. Clarke, 1916.

McMurtry, Larry. *Oh What a Slaughter: Massacres in the American West, 1846–1890*. New York: Simon and Schuster, 2005.

Meredith, Martin. *Coming to Terms: South Africa's Search for Truth*. New York: Public Affairs, 1999.

Merry, Sally Engle. "Kapi'olani at the Brink: Dilemmas of Historical Ethnography in 19th Century Hawai'i." *American Ethnologist* 30, no. 1 (2003): 44–60.

Meyer, Albert L. "San Carlos." In *Annual Report of the Commissioner of Indian Affairs to the Secretary of the Interior for the Year 1896*, 119–123. Washington, D.C.: Government Printing Office, 1896.

Mieder, Wolfgang. "'The Only Good Indian Is a Dead Indian': History and the Meaning of a Proverbial Stereotype." *Journal of American Folklore* 106, no. 419 (1993): 38–60.

Mihesuah, Devon A., ed. *Natives and Academics: Researching and Writing about American Indians*. Lincoln: University of Nebraska Press, 1998.

Minow, Martha. "The Hope for Healing: What Can Truth Commissions Do?" In *Truth v. Justice: The Morality of Truth Commissions*, edited by Robert I. Rotberg and Dennis Thompson, 235–260. Princeton: Princeton University Press, 2000.

Momaday, N. Scott. *The Names: A Memoir*. Tucson: University of Arizona Press, 1976.

Neary, Richard, and David Hoff. *Arizona Military Installations, 1752–1922*. Tempe, Ariz.: Gem Publishing, 1998.

Officer, James E. *Hispanic Arizona, 1536–1856*. Tucson: University of Arizona Press, 1987.

Ogle, Ralph Hendrick. *Federal Control of the Western Apaches, 1848–1886*. Albuquerque: University of New Mexico Press, 1949.

Olwig, Karen F. "The Burden of Heritage: Claiming a Place for a West Indian Culture." *American Ethnologist* 26, no. 2 (1999): 370–388.

O'Neil, Jerry E. "The Camp Grant Massacre." In *Where the Waters Meet: A*

13,000-Year Adventure along the Aravaipa, edited by E. Dean Prichard, 21–25. Winkelman: Central Arizona College, 1985.

Opler, Morris Edward. *An Apache Life-Way: The Economic, Social and Religious Institutions of the Chiricahua Indians*. New York: Cooper Square Publishers, 1965.

Oury, William S. "Historical Truth: The So-Called 'Camp Grant Massacre' of 1871." *Arizona Weekly Star*, July 3, 1879.

———. "Article on Camp Grant Massacre." 1885. Manuscript on file, Arizona Historical Society, Tucson.

Perry, Richard J. *Apache Reservation: Indigenous People and the American State*. Austin: University of Texas Press, 1993.

Pfefferkorn, Ignaz. *Sonora: A Description of the Province*. Albuquerque: University of New Mexico Press, 1949.

Phelps, Teresa Godwin. *Shattered Voices: Language, Violence, and the Work of Truth Commissions*. Philadelphia: University of Pennsylvania Press, 2004.

Plumb, John H. *The Death of the Past*. Boston: Houghton Mifflin, 1970.

Point, Steven L., "Foreword." In *A Stó:lo Coast Salish Historical Atlas*, edited by Keith Thor Carlson, xiii–xv. Vancouver: Douglas & McIntyre, 2001.

Proust, Marcel. *In Search of Lost Time*. Vol. 3, *Guermantes Way*. New York: Random House, 1993.

Record, Ian Wilson. "Aravaipa: Apache Peoplehood and the Legacy of Particular Geography and Historical Experience." PhD diss., American Indian Studies, University of Arizona, 2004.

———. "Extermination versus Reservation: Implications of Civilian Violence against the Apache in the Massacre at Little Running Water (1871)." Master's thesis, American Indian Studies, University of Arizona, 2000.

Rhoades, John D., "The 'Rashomon Effect' Reconsidered." *American Anthropologist* 91, no. 1 (1989): 171.

Robben, Antonius C.G.M. "How Traumatized Societies Remember: The Aftermath of Argentina's Dirty War." *Cultural Critique* 59, no. 1 (2005): 120–164.

Robinson, Sherry. *Apache Voices: Their Stories of Survival as Told to Eva Ball*. Albuquerque: University of New Mexico Press, 2000.

Robinson, W. W., Jr. "Appendix A b, No. 3." In *Annual Report of the Commissioner of Indian Affairs to the Secretary of the Interior for the Year 1871*, 74–76. Washington, D.C.: Government Printing Office, 1872.

Roosevelt, Theodore. *The Winning of the West*. Vol. 3, *The Founding of the Trans-Alleghany*. Lincoln: University of Nebraska Press, 1995.

Rosenzweig, Roy, and David Thalen. *The Presence of the Past: Popular Uses of History in American Life*. New York: Columbia University Press, 1998.

Rotberg, Robert I. "Truth Commissions and the Provision of Truth, Justice, and Reconciliation." In *Truth v. Justice: The Morality of Truth Commis-*

sions, edited by Robert I. Rotberg and Dennis Thompson, 3–21. Princeton: Princeton University Press, 2000.

Russell, Don. "How Many Indians Were Killed? White Man versus Red Man: The Facts and the Legend." *American West,* July 1973, 42–47, 61–63.

Ryden, Don W., and Doug Kupel. "Warfare between Indians and Americans in Arizona, 1846–1886." 1998. Manuscript on file, Arizona State Historic Preservation Office, Phoenix.

Rylko-Bauer, Barbara. "Lessons about Humanity and Survival from My Mother and from the Holocaust." *Anthropological Quarterly* 78, no. 1 (2005): 11–41.

Sahlins, Marshall D. *Historical Metaphors and Mythical Realities: Structure in the Early History of the Sandwich Islands Kingdom.* Ann Arbor: University of Michigan Press, 1981.

Sauer, Carl. "A Spanish Expedition into the Arizona Apacheria." *Arizona Historical Review* 6 (1935): 3–13.

Schellie, Don. *Vast Domain of Blood.* Los Angeles: Westernlore Press, 1968.

Scheper-Hughes, Nancy, and Philippe Bourgois. "Making Sense of Violence." In *Violence in War and Peace,* edited by Nancy Scheper-Hughes and Philippe Bourgois, 1–31. Oxford: Blackwell, 2004.

Schmidt, Peter R., and Thomas C. Patterson, eds. *Making Alternative Histories: The Practice of Archaeology and History in Non-Western Settings.* Santa Fe: School of American Research Press, 1995.

Sedelmayr, Jacobo. *Jacobo Sedelmayr: Missionary, Frontiersman, Explorer in Arizona and Sonora; Four Original Manuscript Narratives, 1744–1751.* Tucson: Arizona Pioneers' Historical Society, 1955.

Sher, George. "Ancient Wrongs and Modern Rights." *Philosophy and Public Affairs* 10, no. 1 (1980): 3–17.

Silko, Leslie Marmon. *Yellow Woman and a Beauty of Spirit: Essays on Native American Life Today.* New York: Touchstone Books, 1996.

Simpson, Moira G. *Making Representations: Museums in the Post-Colonial Era.* London: Routledge Press, 1996.

Smith, Linda Tuhiwai. *Decolonizing Methodologies: Research and Indigenous Peoples.* London: Zed Books, 1999.

Sonnichsen, C. L. *Tucson: The Life and Times of an American City.* Norman: University of Oklahoma Press, 1982.

Spicer, Edward H. *Cycles of Conquest: The Impact of Spain, Mexico, and the United States on the Indians of the Southwest, 1533–1960.* Tucson: University of Arizona Press, 1962.

Spinden, Herbert J. "Myths of the Nez Perce Indians." *Journal of American Folk-lore* 21, no. 2 (1908): 149–158.

Stannard, David E. *American Holocaust: The Conquest of the New World.* Oxford: Oxford University Press, 1992.

Stein, Pat H. "Historic Trails in Arizona from Coronado to 1940: Historic Context Study." 1994. Manuscript on file, Arizona State Historic Preservation Office, Phoenix.

Stone, Jerome Wilson. "The History of Fort Grant." Master's thesis, Department of History, University of Arizona, 1941.

Sweeney, Edwin R. *Cochise: Chiricahua Apache Chief.* Norman: University of Oklahoma Press, 1991.

Thiel, J. Homer, *Beneath the Streets: Prehistoric, Spanish, and American Period Archaeology in Downtown Tucson.* Tucson: Center for Desert Archaeology, 1994.

Thiel, J. Homer, and James M. Vint. "The Life and Times of Santa Cruz de Terrenate." *Archaeology Southwest* 17, no. 3 (2003): 15–16.

Thomas, David Hurst. *Skull Wars: Kennewick Man, Archaeology, and the Battle for Native American Identity.* New York: Basic Books, 2000.

Thomas, Nicholas. "Alejandro Mayta in Fiji: Narratives about Millenarianism, Colonialism, Postcolonial Politics, and Custom." In *Clio in Oceania: Toward a Historical Anthropology,* edited by Alletta Biersack, 297–328. Washington, D.C.: Smithsonian Press, 1991.

Thomas, Robert K. "Papago Land Use: West of the Papago Indian Reservation, South of the Gila River, and the Problem of the Sand Papago Identity." 1963. Manuscript on File, Western Archaeological and Conservation Center Library, Tucson.

Thornton, Thomas F. "Anthropological Studies of Native American Place Naming." *American Indian Quarterly* 21, no. 2 (1997): 209–228.

Thrapp, Dan L. *The Conquest of Apacheria.* Norman: University of Oklahoma Press, 1967.

Tiffany, J. C. "San Carlos." In *Annual Report of the Commissioner of Indian Affairs to the Secretary of the Interior for the Year 1880,* 4–7. Washington, D.C.: Government Printing Office, 1880.

———. "San Carlos." In *Annual Report of the Commissioner of Indian Affairs to the Secretary of the Interior for the Year 1881,* 6–11. Washington, D.C.: Government Printing Office, 1881.

Tinker, George E. *Missionary Conquest: The Gospel and Native American Cultural Genocide.* Minneapolis: Fortress Press, 1993.

Todorov, Tzvetan. *The Conquest of America: The Question of the Other.* New York: Harper and Row, 1984.

Tonkin, Elizabeth. *Narrating Our Pasts: The Social Construction of Oral History.* Cambridge: Cambridge University Press, 1992.

Trafzer, Clifford E. *The Kit Carson Campaign: The Last Great Navajo War.* Norman: University of Oklahoma Press, 1982.

Tutu, Desmond. *No Future without Forgiveness*. New York: Doubleday, 1999.

Underhill, Ruth M. *A Papago Calendar Record*. University of New Mexico Bulletin. Anthropological Series, vol. 2, no. 5 (1938).

———. *Papago Indian Religion*. New York: Columbia University Press, 1946.

———. *Papago Woman*. Prospect Heights, Ill.: Waveland Press, Inc., 1985.

Urla, Jacqueline. "Cultural Politics in an Age of Statistics: Numbers, Nations, and the Making of Basque Identity." *American Ethnologist* 20, no. 4 (1993): 818–843.

Valkenburgh, Richard van. "Apache Ghosts Guard the Aravaipa." *Desert Magazine* 11, no. 6 (1948): 16–20.

Vansina, Jan. *Oral Tradition: A Study in Historical Methodology*. Chicago: Aldine, 1965.

———. *Oral Tradition as History*. Madison: University of Wisconsin Press, 1985.

Vaughn, Stephen. "History: Is It Relevant?" In *The Vital Past: Writings on the Uses of History*, edited by Stephen Vaughn, 1–14. Athens: University of Georgia Press, 1985.

———, ed. *The Vital Past: Writings on the Uses of History*. Athens: University of Georgia Press, 1985.

Volante, Ric. "Massacred Apaches Commemorated." *Arizona Daily Star*, May 1, 1982, 1A.

Waldron, Jeremy. "Superseding Historical Injustice." *Ethics* 103, no. 1 (1992): 4–28.

Wallace, Michael. *Mickey Mouse History and Other Essays on American Memory*. Philadelphia: Temple University Press, 1996.

Wasson, John. "Bloody Retaliation." *Arizona Citizen*, May 6, 1871.

Waterfall, Richard T. "Vengeance at Sunrise: The Camp Grant Massacre, 30 April 1871." *Journal of the West* 21, no. 3 (1992): 110–118.

Watt, Eva Tulene, and Keith H. Basso. *Don't Let the Sun Step Over You: A White Mountain Apache Family Life, 1860–1975*. Tucson: University of Arizona Press, 2004.

Weber, David J. *Myth and the History of the Hispanic Southwest*. Albuquerque: University of New Mexico Press, 1988.

Weissmark, Mona Sue. *Justice Matters: Legacies of the Holocaust and World War II*. Oxford: Oxford University Press, 2004.

Welch, John R. "White Eyes' Lies and the Battle for Dził Nchaa Si'an." *American Indian Quarterly* 21, no. 1 (1997): 75–109.

Welch, John R., and Ramon Riley. "Reclaiming Land and Spirit in the Western Apache Homeland." *American Indian Quarterly* 25, no. 1 (2001): 5–12.

Welch, John R., Chip Colwell-Chanthaphonh, and Mark Altaha. "Retracing the Battle of Cibecue: Western Apache, Documentary, and Archaeological Interpretations." *Kiva* 71, no. 2 (2005): 133–163.

White, Hayden. *Metahistory: The Historical Imagination in Nineteenth-Century Europe*. Baltimore: John Hopkins University Press, 1973.

Whiteley, Peter M. "Archaeology and Oral Tradition: The Scientific Importance of Dialogue." *American Antiquity* 67, no. 3 (2002): 405–415.

Whitman, Royal E. "Appendix A b, No. 2." In *Annual Report of the Commissioner of Indian Affairs to the Secretary of the Interior for the Year 1871*, 69–71. Washington, D.C.: Government Printing Office, 1872.

Wiget, Andrew O. "Recovering the Remembered Past: Folklore and Oral History in the Zuni Trust Lands Damage Case." In *Zuni and the Courts*, edited by Richard E. Hart, 173–187. Lawrence: University Press of Kansas, 1985.

———. "Truth and the Hopi: An Historiographic Study of Documented Oral Tradition Concerning the Coming of the Spanish." *Ethnohistory* 29, no. 3 (1982): 181–199.

Wilson, Roscoe G. "Camp Grant Massacre Called Early State's Most Brutal Tragedy." *Arizona Republic*, July 9, 1950.

Wood, Charles M. "Reminiscences of an Arizona Pioneer." *Tucson Magazine*, November 1953, 22–23.

Worcester, Donald E. *The Apaches: Eagles of the Southwest*. Norman: University of Oklahoma Press, 1979.

Yelvington, Kevin A. "History, Memory, and Identity: A Programmatic Prolegomenon." *Critique of Anthropology* 22, no. 3 (2002): 227–256.

Yoneyama, Lisa. "Traveling Memories, Contagious Justice: Americanization of Japanese War Crimes at the End of the Post–Cold War." *Journal of Asian American Studies* 6, no. 1 (2003): 57–93.

Zerubavel, Yael. *Recovered Roots: Collective Memory and the Making of Israeli National Tradition*. Chicago: University of Chicago Press, 1995.

Zinn, Howard. "What is Radical History?" In *The Vital Past: Writings on the Uses of History*, edited by Stephen Vaughn, 158–169. Athens: University of Georgia Press, 1985.

Figure Credits

Figure 1. Map of the San Pedro Valley. Courtesy of the Center for Desert Archaeology.

Figure 2. The site of the Camp Grant Massacre. Photograph by Chip Colwell-Chanthaphonh, February 18, 2002.

Figure 3. *Haské bahnzin* in 1888. Courtesy of the National Anthropological Archives, Smithsonian Institution; INV 9946000.

Figure 4. Chiquito and his wife in 1876. Courtesy of the National Anthropological Archives, Smithsonian Institution; INV 02031900.

Figure 5. Map of places Walter Hooke traveled. Courtesy of the Center for Desert Archaeology.

Figure 6. Map of places *bija gush kaiyé* traveled. Courtesy of the Center for Desert Archaeology.

Figure 7. San Carlos Apache elder Jeanette Cassa. Photograph by T. J. Ferguson, January 24, 2003.

Figure 8. Map of clan migrations and Aravaipa and Pinal band territories. Courtesy of the Center for Desert Archaeology; Adapted from Goodwin 1942:Map I, Map VI.

Figure 9. Camp Grant in 1871. Photograph by Timothy O'Sullivan, from the series Geographic Explorations and Surveys West of the 100th Meridian, 1871–1874, National Archives at College Park, Maryland, 106-WB-100.

Figure 10. Timing of raiding and rationing in April 1871. Courtesy of the Center for Desert Archaeology.

Figure 11. Map of Apache farms near Dudleyville in 1885. Courtesy of the Center for Desert Archaeology; adapted from Plat Showing Location of Indian

Settlements on the San Pedro River, Pinal County, Arizona / Surveyed by George J. Roskruge Under Instructions from F.E. Pierce; Arizona Historical Society/Tucson, G4332.S2 G46, 1885, R6.

Figure 12. Map showing Chiquito's farm. Courtesy of the Center for Desert Archaeology. Adapted from Survey Plat, Township 7S, Range 17E, Gila-Salt Meridian, Arizona, Officially Filed April 8, 1907, Survey General's Office; Bureau of Land Management, Phoenix.

Figure 13. Stevenson Talgo and Howard Hooke. Photograph by T. J. Ferguson, January 3, 2003.

Figure 14. The cover of *Embrace the Wind*. Courtesy of Chelley Kitzmiller.

Index

About the Author

Chip Colwell-Chanthaphonh, born and raised in Tucson, Arizona, received his BA in anthropology from the University of Arizona in 1996 and his doctorate in anthropology from Indiana University in 2004. He is the author of *History Is in the Land: Multivocal Tribal Traditions in Arizona's San Pedro Valley* (with T. J. Ferguson) and co-editor of *Archaeological Ethics* (with Karen D. Vitelli). He has also published in numerous journals, including *American Anthropologist, American Indian Quarterly, History and Anthropology, Journal of Social Archaeology, Kiva,* and *Journal of the Southwest.* Dr. Colwell-Chanthaphonh wrote this book as a Fellow at the Center for Desert Archaeology in Tucson and later as a Visiting Scholar at the American Academy of Arts & Sciences in Cambridge, Massachusetts. He is now the Project Director at Anthropological Research, LLC.